OTHER BOOKS

QUANTUM SELF HYPNOSIS

QUANTUM HYPNOSIS SCRIPTS

BLUEPRINT FOR HAPPINESS

EYES OPEN SELF HYPNOSIS

An Uncommon Guide to Getting Thin, Getting Happy and Getting More!

Jo Ana Starr, PhD

The Publishing Group Inc

USA

TABLE OF CONTENTS

CHAPTER 1-INTRODUCTION 7

CHAPTER 2-THE POWER OF YOUR MIND 21

CHAPTER 3-THE MAGIC OF EOSH 33

CHAPTER 4-HYPNOTIC NARRATIVES 47

CHAPTER 5-HYPNOTIC DECLARATIONS 213

CHAPTER 6-MAXIMIZE YOUR SUCCESS 271

CHAPTER 1

INTRODUCTION

I believe in you. I believe in the infinite power of your human mind and spirit. I believe that you are truly limitless and capable of creating the life of your dreams. By buying this book you have demonstrated a belief in the possibility of creating the life that you want, and this first powerful step moves you closer to your goal! I believe that any person who makes a "true decision" and who employs an effective method to harness the power of his mind can accomplish miracles!

By using EOSH, you can make any behavioral change you truly desire. I wrote this book to share with you an easy and effective method to create a happier life for you and those around you. I hope you enjoy *Eyes Open Self Hypnosis* and use what you learn to create exactly what you desire. In this book, you will find 30 ready-to-use, right out of the box

EOSH Primary Sessions and another 58 EOSH Bonus Sessions, so in combination with the provided General Primary Session Template you can create another 58 sessions giving you a total of 88 Eyes Open Self Hypnosis Sessions covering the areas of Career, Relationship and General categories.

All readers receive a FREE audio Eyes Open Self Hypnosis Primary Session, so you can experience the best way to use your sessions. An EOSH audio session is a shorter Self Hypnosis session, so you will find the cadence relaxing and enjoyable. More information on your free session can be found in the last chapter.

This book was inspired by my ongoing personal research into the best ways to create quick and effective personal change. As a Certified Clinical Hypnotherapist and trainer of 27 years, as well as a devoted explorer of mind-body technologies, I have found Self Hypnosis to be the easiest and most effective way to create behavioral change. The downsides are few, so few in fact that I've never really considered them more than minor inconveniences. Here's what I mean. Traditional Self Hypnosis requires a little bit of technology such as a sound recorder and the willingness to create a few audio files or CDs for your use. Then there is a daily time requirement of about 45 minutes, which is still doable for most. That daily commitment is a consideration. Considering what can be gained by using tradition Self Hypnosis, these are really minor inconveniences on the path to dynamic and permanent change!

I have learned from the growing readership of both *Quantum Self Hypnosis* and *Quantum Hypnosis Scripts* that there is an enormous interest in Self Hypnosis among individuals who are seeking the most effective method to create desired changes in their lives. And for most of them, with traditional Self Hypnosis they've found the perfect way to make those changes. People love Self Hypnosis because it works, it's cheap, and the sessions are really enjoyable. For those who love the DIY approach, Self Hypnosis is a powerful, affordable way to reprogram beliefs and thus change behavior. And for those who don't, there are thousands of practicing

Certified Hypnotherapists around the world ready and willing to help you.

So, what are these downsides to traditional Self Hypnosis that I alluded to earlier? Those using traditional Self Hypnosis need to be able to record sessions and to play them daily for a month or so. The sessions are between 30-45 minutes long which is a relatively short period of time, but for some individuals finding 30 minutes of quiet time daily can be a challenge. Many peoples live full lives brimming over with personal responsibilities, work, family, etc. This daily time requirement may be more daunting for some Self Hypnotists than even the recording part of the process.

So what's the solution? As I mentioned earlier, I am no stranger to any of the mind-body practices and technologies. I was there in the 70's using creative visualization, affirmations, guided imagery, Silva in the 80's, light and sound machines in the 90's, meditation, etc. Until I found Self Hypnosis, I continued to feel that the perfect solution in the quest for personal growth and personal change was evading me. With Hypnosis, I felt that I had finally found a way to achieve deeper and more permanent change than I had with previous methods. Don't misunderstand me. We're all different and what is perfect for one person may not be perfect for the next person, but that said, even compared to Silva which I loved and found very effective, I realized that Hypnosis was my true, final solution. Quick, no side effects and lots of unexpected side benefits, Hypnosis and Self Hypnosis provided me and my clients with amazing, super-speedy results reliably and pleasantly. So, yes, I do love and believe in the processes of Hypnosis and traditional Self Hypnosis. As a way to modify limiting beliefs and to institute fairly effortless behavioral change, without drugs, machines, and hours of work, Self Hypnosis is hard to beat. Of course, when I first fell in love with the process of Hypnosis, we were all living in a different world, pre-Internet, pre-cell phones, etc. The world was a slower place back then. Today's pace is daunting, and sometimes finding a free hour daily can be challenging. Fortunately, busy or technology-challenged individuals will find the Eyes Open Self

Hypnosis method that I share with you in this book to be a great solution delivering permanent, dynamic change with a very small daily time requirement.

To offer an historical perspective, here are some of the other methods that utilize the mind-body connection in ways that are somewhat similar to Self Hypnosis, although not as effective, in my opinion. Some of these methods you have investigated or may have tried. Here's my take on these other methods for self-change:

OTHER MIND-BODY METHODS:

AFFIRMATIONS

Affirmations are positive statements repeated throughout the day; they are easy to use and can help to break that negative tape that many people unknowingly play in their heads, but used alone for behavioral change, I have found them to be ineffective and to take as much or more time than traditional Self Hypnosis minus the power of the Subconscious mind. You carry a card with 4 or 5 positive statements and repeat them to yourself in spare moments, such as driving the car, washing the dishes, etc. I feel that traditional affirmations work best at occupying the mind with positive thoughts, instead of negative self-talk, so used for that purpose they are wonderful!

CREATIVE VISUALIZATION

Creative visualization can be used in a way that's similar to traditional Self Hypnosis. The user images in the conscious state with his eyes closed, a situation or event in which he is doing sometime that he'd like to experience in the real world. Creative visualization is also used in a guided meditation format which is similar to a Self Hypnosis session but which doesn't cause the participant to go deeply enough into a meditative state to fully engage the Subconscious Mind. This process requires almost as much daily time as Self Hypnosis sessions but typical doesn't empower the Subconscious Mind which is the key to creating permanent behavioral change. This method, much like the use of affirmations alone, does absolutely no harm and can help an individual to create a more positive outlook toward a situation, another individual or an event. It's kind of like Self Hypnosis without the oomph.

LIGHT - SOUND MACHINES

These small devices can be fun to experience if you're into the mind-body thing. These machines use flashing lights and often a measured beat that plays through speakers with the beats synchronized with the flashing lights. The purpose is to entrain the brain to enter a more relaxed or a different brain state. Personally I had trouble with the flashing lights which made me feel quite anxious. I tried different colored lights but still these machines were anything but relaxing for me. Although I am not epileptic, I later read that Epileptics shouldn't use these machines as they can induce seizures, so anyone reading this with any brain imbalance should proceed with caution when using these machines. While they aren't terribly expensive, a mid-range device is priced around $200, so they aren't inexpensive either.

In terms of our discussion, these machines are not designed to do anything other than relax the individual by pacing the brain, thus causing it to enter an alpha or another brain state. These devices are not designed to change beliefs or specific behaviors so they are not really an alternate to Self Hypnosis. I included this category just for the reader's edification and because the use of these devices does fall within the mind-body field.

NLP

NLP stands for Neuro-linguistic Programming. The self-use of NLP involves quite a bit of training to use this modality fully. Whether you are a proponent of NLP or not, everyone can benefit by learning the different states of learning and communication that are the hallmarks of NLP, as well as well as behavior modulating components like pacing and mirroring. These are powerful tools that can really enhance the process of communicating with others and they are valuable for that reason.

This really interesting modality was developed by two gentlemen named Bandler and Grinder and became popularized by Tony Robbins. Tony simplified the basic techniques and the original information to make it much more accessible for everyone. Tony has written a few really wonderful books on the subject and he offers his audio training programs and seminars internationally.

There is a considerable time commitment involved in grasping more than the basics of NLP, and frankly without Tony's programs or others like his, it can be difficult to fully implement. I use aspects of NLP in the NEIH training programs and have read several of Tony's books with great interest and used his audio programs.

As compared with Self Hypnosis, NLP has a much longer learning curve and frankly and the process of NLP does not access the Subconscious Mind. NLP is a conscious state learning tool and as such, is not as fast or effective as Self Hypnosis for behavioral change, based on my personal experience. However, learning the key components of NLP is extremely valuable for those who want to develop excellent communication skills.

Please be clear. I am not being critical of NLP or Tony, whom I believe has helped many hundreds of thousands of people to defeat depression and to begin taking positive actions to improve their lives. I admire him enormously and consider him a great humanitarian and role model for us all. If you've attended any of his events or seen him on TV, it's clear that he's a remarkable human being. But NLP without Tony or another skilled NLP practitioner can be a bit challenging to use on your own. And again, the use of NLP does not access your Subconscious Mind which is NLP's greatest weakness. If you've ever tried to stop smoking by making a conscious state decision, you know what I mean. The conscious state mind is all about maintaining the status quo not about creating change.

There are a few other methods for creating behavioral changes such as Biofeedback devices not normally available to untrained prospective users, counseling, energy work, and more. I believe based on years of personal research that the easiest and most powerful modality to create change is Self Hypnosis because the use of Self Hypnosis is the easiest way to access your inner genius, your subconscious mind.

So what is this subconscious mind I keep referring to? The subconscious mind is the aspect of mind which is the most creative, changeable, and versatile, unlike the conscious mind which is designed to maintain the status quo. When you write a poem or a brilliant blog entry, you are accessing your subconscious mind. When you paint a picture, frame the perfect photo shot, design a room, or create a fabulous recipe, you are using your subconscious mind. Your subconscious mind is child-like and creative; it loves sound, color, symbols, images, and variety and it's analogous to the Right Brain. The subconscious mind's job is to create, while the conscious mind's job is to organize, verbalize, and to maintain everything just as it is in a state called homeostasis. It's easy to see why trying to use the conscious mind to change isn't effective as change is the exact opposite of maintaining the status quo.

The conscious mind doesn't like change and resists. The subconscious mind, however, loves change and loves to learn, so that particular mind-state facilitates change easily. Accessing the subconscious mind to create behavioral changes or to upgrade existing beliefs is like filling your car with premium gasoline; you're going to get where you want to be as quickly as possible. Trying to force the conscious mind to accept change is like forgetting to put gas in the car before a road trip; those gas fumes at the bottom of the gas tank aren't going to get you very far. It's so much more effective to use the part of your mind that loves change to affect change, isn't it? And that's the magic of Self Hypnosis. It allows you easy access to your Subconscious Mind where change occurs so easily. The use of Self Hypnosis for change is the perfect way to access your inner "change" genius, your subconscious mind. Now let's take a look at that wonderful, magical mind that you have!

CHAPTER 2

THE POWER OF YOUR MIND

We touched on the power of your mind in the first chapter, and I'd like to spend a bit more time familiarizing you with that amazing real estate you carry around with you every day. I have often said and completely believe that per square inch, your brain is the most valuable piece of real estate on the planet, at least as it relates to you and the quality of your life!

We've talked a bit about both the conscious and the subconscious minds in the first chapter. We will look at these in more detail shortly. Right now, I'd like to share the idea of Brain as separate from Mind. Aren't the terms "brain" and "mind" synonymous? Well, for a long time, they were believed to be the same, both residing in your head, occupying exactly the same space. Your brain is definitely in your head, but Mind is everywhere in your body. The concept of Mind as part of every cell in your body is a fairly new one. We will examine aspects of mind as cellular intelligence next.

Each cell in your body has measurable intelligence and is capable of communicating with every other cell in your body, and not just as a function of the autonomous nervous system. Deepak Chopra has spoken at length on this subject in several of his books. He believes based on research conducted around the world that each cell in our bodies has cellular intelligence and is capable of communicating with every other cell, and does. Let's look at the Heart as an example of cellular communication. That familiar quandary as to whether you should think with your heart or your head is actually more of a choice than any of us thought. The heart is now believed to have as much measurable intelligence as your brain, as revealed by the HeartMath organization. A US non profit organization, the Institute of HeartMath, has found that the heart has 40,000 neurons (the same number in the brain itself), and the intuitive signals the heart sends, including feelings of love, happiness, care, and appreciation are expression of the heart's intelligence, changing the nervous system in ways that allow for greater production of DHEA, the so-called "fountain of youth" hormone. Amazing. We've all known that the heart pumps blood throughout our bodies, but it also is now known as a major intelligence conduit.

Not only do our cells communicate with each other, but parasitic organisms living in our bodies communicate with us in ways that influence our behavior. Scientists have discovered the somewhat disturbing information that parasites residing in human beings can influence their hosts' minds to consume foods that nourish the parasites. They are also believed to influence other behaviors in their hosts, us! When you get a strong craving for something you know isn't good for you, pause for a second and consider that you may not be the originator of that craving - tiny parasitic creatures may be signaling your body-mind that they need more food. If that's not enough to put you off sweets and yeasts, I don't know what is. The good news is that if tiny parasitic creatures can communication with our minds, then imagine how much easier it is for our own cells to communicate among themselves.

Check below for more information on inter-species communication between toxoplasma and their human hosts:

http://www.theatlantic.com/magazine/archive/2012/03/how-your-cat-is-making-you-crazy/8873/

Candace Pert, author of *Molecules of Emotion: Why You Feel the Way You Feel*, agrees with the growing belief in cellular intelligence and tells her readers that mind is not separate from body...mind infuses the body. She has determined that an information transfer system beginning at the cellular level operates throughout the body coordinating physiology, behavior and emotion in a coherent manner. Emma Bragdon, PhD summarizes some of the author's work on cellular intelligence research here:

http://www.emmabragdon.com/articles/art-09.html

So, humans are blessed with cellular intelligence and probably, "mind" as we perceive it in every cell of our bodies. Amazing!

Let's get back to the Conscious Mind and the Subconscious Mind constructs for a moment. For those of you who have read books on Hypnosis or taken trainings that refer to the "Unconscious Mind"; this is a misnomer. There is no such thing as an "unconscious mind" in a conscious individual. An unconscious mind is a mind that exists in an unconscious person, someone who has lost consciousness. In a conscious human, there are only the conscious mind and the subconscious mind states. Whether you consider this a fine point or a big deal as I do, the topic of the subconscious mind is central to this book. Let's call it what it is.

Let's go back to the brain. Humans have a brain which is compartmentalized as a left brain which is analogous to the conscious mind in terms of types of functioning and a right brain that is analogous to the subconscious mind in terms of types of functioning. Within the brain, there is a tiny bridge that connects the left and right hemispheres of the human brain, thus uniting the separate sides of the brain commonly referred to as the left brain and the right brain.

Typical left brain (conscious mind) functioning is verbal, organizational, mathematical, and logical.

Typical right brain functioning (subconscious mind) is non-verbal, creative, emotive, playful, visual and auditory. The perfectly beautiful balance of the two hemispheres of the brain is amazing. This tiny bridge allows humans to jump from a predominantly left brain day of balancing checkbooks to a fun, unplanned special meal utilizing right brain function to whip up a whole new take on an old family favorite, seamlessly. And that same lovely right brain is used by every Self Hypnotist who creates and uses his own Self Hypnosis audio file or CD. If he types a script that he has created, he is using both his left and right brain simultaneously.

Working humans in this era engage primarily in left brain activities; not all people certainly, but arguably a majority of them. Most work activities are logical, left brain and organizational, causing a marked imbalance in brain hemisphere use for most people in developed nations. And as you have probably figured out by now, right brain activities are much more fun, more nourishing and relaxing than left brain activities for most people. One of the major bonuses for any serious Self Hypnotist is the opportunity to establish a more balanced use of both hemispheres of the brain. And while a Self Hypnosis session may not be as much fun as a day at Disney World, in terms of relaxation, stress relief, healing and balanced brain use, it probably feels like more fun to your body. Thirty minutes a day of yoga, meditation, or self hypnosis is believed to add years to your life, and to improve the quality of every day of your life. The benefits of these activities very likely outweigh the effort or time involved.

Now that you are beginning to understand the differences between brain and mind, and the general functioning of each hemisphere of the brain, we can move on the heart of the matter. Your brilliant mind is capable of creating miracles in your life or disasters in your life. Your brilliant mind is like a sponge, soaking up information at every turn. You are influenced by everything you hear, everything you see and everything you say. Please think about this because Hypnosis is occurring all the time. Long before you engage in your first Eyes Open Self Hypnosis session, you will have been exposed to thousands of hours of Hypnosis or mental programming.

When you were still a child, you learned much of what you "know" today. What you learned may not have been positive. You may have learned that you're not very bright, not very pretty, not very easy to deal with, unlikely to succeed, etc. These things aren't true because you are who you decide that you are; your future is not determined by your genomes or your upbringing, but by whom you decide to be. I'm not suggesting that it will be easy or instant to become the perfect version of you, but it's not rocket science either, nor is it expensive to accomplish enormous, positive changes in your life. It just takes commitment and some time. You already have the most important tools in your toolbox: a genius brain, a mind and a body. With those three things, you can be whomever you decide to be. Granted, if you're 5 feet tall and you want to be 6 feet tall, you may have to settle a bit in that area, but in terms of personality, energy level, appearance, weight, open-heartedness, spirituality, kindness, wellness, love, self esteem, success and so many other choices, you are in

28

control. If you're shaking your head, just stop for a minute. Pretend what I've said is true. If you pretended it was true and invested a month to find out, what could you possibly lose? So, yes, you would expose yourself to the possibility of disappointment, but the payoff could be amazing! And you wouldn't be alone. There are so many people in our society who have pulled themselves up by the bootstraps and become the persons they pictured themselves becoming.

I know you've been subject to a lot of societal and familial hypnotic influences that may have persuaded you that you are much less powerful than you actually are. I covered those hypnotic influences in detail in *Quantum Self Hypnosis,* so I'm not going to spend much time on them here. Trust me. You, just like every human on the planet, is a unique, infinitely powerful, potentially amazing person. Right now you are using about 5% of your brain's cognitive capacity and probably getting along pretty well. Wouldn't it be nice to learn how to access another 5% of that big brain of yours? It's sitting there waiting to be activated more fully, and doing so will improve the quality of your life to an astonishing degree.

Unfortunately, your family and your schools may have taught you not to think and if that's so, you can release that "learning" very shortly and just think, think, think!! This statement isn't intended as a slam against schools or your family, but as a person who was "trained" by both family and public schools, I know that the statement is true. We are trained to follow, not to think. We are trained to listen to the general consensus, accept it as true, and act on it. Well, you know what they say about the masses. God gave you both a brain and a mind to create goodness in the world and in your life. Do not accept the limitations that society or group consciousness places on you. You are here for greatness; embrace your true potential by using your mind as effectively as you can.

I write books that teach people how to get what they want, by using what they already have.....a big brain, a mind and a body. You don't need a college education, nor do you need a high school education to become exactly who you want to be. If you only get free of that societal bias by reading this book, it will have been worth it for you. It's time to release the limitations that other people and society may have placed on you. You're plenty smart enough to get what you want, and you're more than good looking enough. If you don't believe me, go online and pull up the photos of some of the most successful people in the world. Then go look at yourself in the mirror! See what I mean! As far as smart enough goes, kicking your brain usage up just 1 percentage point will super-charge your life.

Here are a few great ways to kick your brain into a higher gear. If you've always been a follower, try being a leader just once. You may totally love it! If you're in a rut, get out of it; take any new action that will propel you into a new experience and get you out of that rut. The point is, your life is in your hands. The limitations you embrace become your life. Choose to become limitless!

The bottom line is this. You have everything you need to achieve whatever you want. Using what you already have and adding Eyes Open Self Hypnosis, which is a time-conserving version of Self Hypnosis, will help you to transform your life.

Eyes Open Self Hypnosis is a new form of Self Hypnosis that allows you to integrate the power of Self Hypnosis into your life in two to eight minute chunks of time daily.

In this chapter, we covered the Brain/Mind parallel, the Subconscious Mind, the Conscious Mind, alternate methods for change, cellular communication and finally the incredible power of your mind. We're there. On to this really effective, new Self Hypnosis approach, Eyes Open Self Hypnosis!

CHAPTER 3

THE MAGIC OF EYES OPEN SELF HYPNOSIS

First of all, the process of Eyes Open Self Hypnosis harnesses the power of traditional Self Hypnosis in two ways, by creating a heightened focus on the ideal outcome and by creating a lighter, easy to attain state of Hypnosis. Is this state as deep a state as achieved in traditional Self Hypnosis? At first, using EOSH produces a very light state of Hypnosis in most users which deepens fairly quickly with repeated use. Even in the beginning, some individuals reach a more traditional state of Hypnosis. It depends on the individual. The amount of time needed will differ with each individual, based on many factors such as, his previous experience with altered states, his motivation, and whether he uses the EOSH sessions at least daily, and so on. Let's look at traditional Self Hypnosis briefly, since the goal of EOSH is to provide the benefits of traditional Self Hypnosis with less effort and less time.

Self Hypnosis is a hypnotic method that employs a traditional Hypnosis script which is read and recorded by the Self-Hypnotist, and then listened to daily. For those who have the time and willingness to record a session and play it daily, I believe that traditional Self Hypnosis is the fastest way to create behavioral change. That daily dose of 45 minutes of Hypnosis is a powerful tool in creating life change and as of the moment, it's the best method I've experienced. That said, if an individual doesn't make or find the time to record his session, or if he's anxious about the process for some reason and doesn't begin, then he's not experiencing Self Hypnosis at all. Many people believe in the power of Self Hypnosis and plan to use it when time becomes available, and unfortunately that day never seems to come. Self Hypnosis books are read and the plan to record a session is delayed which is unfortunate, but understandable. There are still only 24 hours in the day and if those hours are already committed, then optional activities have to be postponed.

In contrast, Eyes Open Self Hypnosis is very user friendly, seems natural to the beginning user, and takes very little time. If an individual can find the time to review a fairly short Primary EOSH session daily, he is on his way to personal change. Adding the Bonus sessions daily makes the EOSH program even more effective. The use of Eyes Open Self Hypnosis allows just about anyone to begin a program that will offer many benefits with a tiny time commitment. The daily use of EOSH provides the needed focus to create change; and in a short period of time, the hypnotic effects of repeated use of the EOSH Primary and Bonus sessions will provide increased relaxation, as well as the changes that the EOSH participant desires.

Positive focus on an ideal outcome or goal can be challenging for those of us living in a developed nation, and it's critical to focus on the desired outcome to achieve it. We have too many choices and often too many daily chores. The average US citizen has in excess of 5000 thoughts a day and makes more than 50 decisions a day. I know that sounds like a lot, but think about an average morning is which you decide what to wear, what to have for breakfast, whether to have breakfast, outlining what you have to do today and deciding when to do which task, etc. Your brain is hard at work 24 hours a day working on a very diverse number of tasks. Is there a downside to having all these daily thoughts and decisions? Absolutely! They create a lack of focus on what you really want in your life, or perhaps I should say that they break focus. And positive focus on the ideal outcome is essential to manifest what you want.

Let's say that you want a new job. You may think about the current job as a negative, and place focus on how much you dislike the current job and yet believe that you are focusing on manifesting a better one. Unfortunately, the way your subconscious mind works is that: whatever you focus on sufficiently, you will create more of in your life. So if you focus on disliking your current job, you are actually reducing the likelihood that you will attract another one because your focus is on disliking this current job. If you add in an emotional soup of dislike, resentment, and anger, these powerful energetic emotions can actually attract what you are choosing to leave behind. Using EOSH allows you to refocus your mind on whatever changes you want to occur in your life. The EOSH approach to wanting to attract a new job would be to cease reacting to or even actively disliking the old job; and instead placing all mental focus on the desired, ideal job. Focusing on the positive aspects of the job you'd like to have will help to manifest an ideal job. This basic concept applies to every change you'd like to make in your life, not just getting a new job. Attracting a mate, improving relationships with siblings or friends, developing more self-confidence are just a few of the many wonderful improvements you can make in your life, just by using your genius mind more effectively.

If you want to find a husband, telling yourself and anyone who will listen that all the good men are taken, is pretty counter-productive. An EOSH session would focus on the type of husband you'd like, and celebrate the fact that there are so many good men out there just looking for a woman like you. Keeping a positive focus on your ideal outcome is a powerful way to attract that outcome to you. I am the first to admit that making these changes in thinking can be a bit of a challenge, particularly at

37

first. Everyone has non-productive verbalizations that slip off the tongue because they have been repeated so often. Even well into an EOSH program, you will occasionally shock yourself by speaking aloud, one of the expressions that used to be part of your conversational repertoire. The power of repeatedly saying and hearing a particular phrase is undeniable, so make sure the phrases and sentences that come out of your mouth fully support your goal. It may require some discipline to on your part, particularly if you have become accustomed to complaining aloud about the things in life that annoy you. My advice would be to consciously listen to every word that comes out of your mouth and to stop saying words and sentences that don't support your stated goals. The good news is that giving up on complaining will speed wonderful new opportunities into your life. Positivity is the key. Speak and hear only that which you want to show up in your life. That one change alone will reward you grandly.

The basis for life change is simple whether you're using EOSH, traditional Self Hypnosis, or another method. As you change your thinking and your vocalizing, your life changes. And you create change by focusing on the desired result, not the undesired present circumstances. If you focus on what exists and what's wrong with it, you will get more of that. If you focus on the new, improved version of your life that you can see in your mind's eye, you will attract that life to you. And given all the daily thoughts and decisions that most individuals engage in, focus can only be fully achieved through concerted efforts, ideally using a method that employs the genius of your subconscious mind. Eyes Open Self Hypnosis or traditional Self Hypnosis both activate your subconscious mind and provide increased, positive focus on the desired life changes as well as a sunnier outlook on your present circumstances. A happy side benefit of either of these approaches is increased relaxation and general well-being.

One big advantage of EOSH over traditional Self Hypnosis is this. If you find yourself in a situation that honestly feels worthy of complaint, you can pull out your EOSH Bonus Session and use it to remind yourself that the current circumstances are changing;

you can choose not to empower the current situation by supercharging it with negative emotion. Pretend you are Superman or Superwoman, incapable of being annoyed. Bite the bullet and smile, smile, smile. It's interesting to note that when annoying people don't get a reaction from others, they frequently find that being annoying isn't worth the effort. A phrase I read years ago that has proven true in my life describes this situation I just mentioned. "You attract what you resist." Again, negative, angry energy is pretty powerful and can attract exactly what you don't want in your life. Focusing anger or any negativity on any situation, intensifies the situation instead of improving it.

If you find yourself in an unpleasant situation, you can take the long view that the current situation is temporary and frankly not worth getting an ulcer over. When you stop reacting to an unpleasant situation, the world around you changes for the better.

One of the major benefits of using EOSH is that it allows you to begin to comprehend how much control or power you have over current situations, whether work or family or anything else in your life. The power of your subconscious mind kicks in more often and you begin to see yourself not as an occasional victim of "fate", but as the architect of your life, which attitude can be very empowering. When you begin to experience how much your thinking can change the external circumstances of your life, you realize how completely you are creating your current life. And with that realization comes the next realization which is this: if you created the current one, you can re-create a better one. Allow yourself to savor, just for a moment, the possibility that in your current life, you have an almost endless number of possible do-overs. If the current life isn't exactly what you want, then decide what your ideal life is and use EOSH to reinforce your focus on attracting your ideal life, no longer energetically blocking it. I know that sentence was a mouthful, but read it again. I believe that Spirit, God or your Higher Self is just waiting for clear instructions on exactly what you want in your life. I also believe that the lack of focus on the desired outcome sends mixed messages out to the Universe and blocks our achieving the lives that we desire. With EOSH, we are able to focus our minds on what we want and to re-focus during the day as often as we like.

Eyes Open Self Hypnosis is simple, and works like this. The EOSH participant uses his Primary session daily in under 10 minutes and reinforces it several times daily with the EOSH Bonus sessions. The EOSH primary session anchors-in very positive feelings about the subject-topic and begins the Hypnotic process. The Bonus sessions reinforce that feeling and constantly refocus the mind. The EOSH Bonus session uses the hypnotic suggestions in the EOSH Primary session and re-awakens the feelings experienced in the primary EOSH session, thus reinforcing the ideal outcome. The use of the EOSH bonus sessions seems to change the tone of the moment in which they are used. So, again, if you find yourself in a negative-feeling situation at work or elsewhere, take a moment for an EOSH bonus session break. Doing so will often remind you of the truth; you've made a decision about the life you want and anything that distracts from that doesn't matter. Your positive focus on your end-game is what matters; recapture that focus and allow a less than ideal moment to pass, without anger or any other negative reactions.

This is a simple, right out-of-the-box, effective method for self-change. In the beginning, however, it is important to commit to changing embedded patterns of reaction and behavior. It takes a bit of control to smile when you want to hiss. It can take some effort to take a deep breath and choose not to react. Doing so, with the assistance of EOSH primary and bonus sessions, will reward you with a better life - less upset, more certainty, more confidence and a much greater sense of well-being. And ultimately, when you're ready, you will find yourself suddenly confronting a fabulous job offer, a great relationship, a healthier body, or whatever your first EOSH project will be. Have patience, keep doing the "work" and keep a hopeful eye out for signs of your desired outcome!

By now you must be curious to know what an EOSH Primary session comprises, so I'm going to address that right now. In traditional Self Hypnosis, a hypnotic induction and a hypnosis script are read aloud, recorded, and then played by the Self-Hypnotist, daily if possible. In an EOSH primary session, a hypnotic narrative is either created or one of the EOSH hypnotic narratives included in this book is used. The narrative resembles a Self Hypnosis script in certain ways. Like a hypnosis script, the EOSH narrative is present tense, positive, and slightly cadenced, although much shorter than a traditional Self Hypnosis script and less cadenced. There's no traditional hypnotic induction count-down in the EOSH primary session, although there is a narrative section that suggests increased relaxation and increased suggestibility. The total time needed to slowly review the EOSH primary session, either aloud or silently, is less than 10 minutes. We encourage those using an EOSH primary session not to rush. Although the primary EOSH session doesn't require the use of a traditional cadence, a slower reading of the primary EOSH session will be more effective for most EOSH participants.

The EOSH Bonus session is a short list of key points or suggestions that are addressed in the EOSH Primary session. The Bonus session acts to reinforce the purpose of your current EOSH program. It takes about a minute or two to review a few hypnotic suggestions and to allow yourself to visualize in your mind's eye some aspect of your ideal outcome. If imaging is challenging for you at first, it's okay. Just use these minutes to think about how nice it will be for you when you've accomplished your goals. Just let yourself feel the pleasure of achieving your outcome.

That's pretty much it. EOSH completely demystifies Self Hypnosis and makes it easy and fully achievable for anyone who can read, to create positive, measurable change in their lives. There's nothing difficult or odd about EOSH, although in fairness, I don't think there's anything odd about Self Hypnosis either, but that's me. I have worked in this field for

26 years, so these processes seem as natural to me as taking a breath.

So that's the general how and why of Eyes Open Self Hypnosis. The process is uncomplicated and easy for anyone to use. And even though so little time is needed daily as compared with traditional Self Hypnosis, it's important to find the time to use the Primary and Bonus sessions daily. The daily use of EOSH can help anyone to achieve his ideal outcome.

CHAPTER 4

EYES OPEN SELF HYPNOTIC NARRATIVES

This chapter provides you with a Primary EOSH Session Template which when combined with your Bonus Session declarations or your own DYI declarations makes it possible to create an infinite number of EOSH Primary sessions; as well as 30 ready-to-use complete Primary Sessions.

OK. Let's get started. Below we've included the best way to begin to use your first EOSH Primary session!

Getting Ready to Use Your First EOSH Primary Session

The terms EOSH Primary Session and EOSH Hypnotic Narrative are used synonymously in this book, so don't be confused by the chapter title. This chapter provides you with all the tools you need to use the ready-to-use EOSH primary sessions or to begin to create your own.

To begin, find a quiet spot where you can speak aloud or read quietly for about 8 minutes. You don't need to be alone, but you do need to feel comfortable enough to allow yourself to enter a very relaxed state as you read your Hypnotic Narrative.

There may be an advantage to reviewing the EOSH primary session aloud, particularly if you enjoy listening to music, audio training programs, etc. This may indicate that you are an auditory learner, so hearing the session might heighten the impact for you. Whether reading aloud or silently, you will accumulate added benefits every time you use your primary EOSH session, so don't worry. Try speaking it aloud one day and the next time review your session silently to see which you prefer. Either method will reward you grandly!

If you have a lot of experience with meditation, guided imagery, and self hypnosis, you will feel increasing relaxation as soon as you begin to review your first EOSH primary session. If this is new to you, be patient with yourself and with the process, and expect very quickly to enjoy the benefits of increased relaxation and increased focus on your goal. Expect even quicker results as you become accustomed to the process.

EOSH PRIMARY SESSION HYPNOTIC NARRATIVE TEMPLATE

This is a Template you can use in two ways. You can create 58 additional Primary EOSH Sessions by adding the Bonus Session declarations listed in Chapter 5 to this template. Adding the declarations to the template in the areas listed below as [Add Hypnotic Affirmation Here] or [Affirmation Here] or [Add Title of Hypnotic Affirmation] creates a new EOSH Primary Session. You can also create an unlimited number of DYI session-topics if you choose, by writing your own hypnotic declarations and then adding them to this Primary Session Template.

Read your selected Primary Session slowly, in a slightly cadenced way. Doing so will be easier after you listen to the Free Primary EOSH General Session that you can download at http://eyesopenselfhypnosis.com. Play the downloaded audio several times to begin the hypnotic process and to make using your own Primary Session easier.

The EOSH Primary Session Hypnotic Narrative Template follows:

Breathing deeply, I relax my shoulders, my jaw, and the corners of my mouth. My hands feel pleasantly heavy and I lay them on my knees. I can feel how heavy they seem. I breathe deeply and imagine my life as a canvas on which I will be painting today. I can imagine painting the beautiful picture that my life can be.

I believe that I am empowered to create miracles in my life. As I accept this, that reality awakens and begins to form as part of my belief system. I imagine how good it feels to be a magnet for all good things, all good events and all good people. I allow myself to sense how happy I am becoming, as a person whose energy attracts all goodness to myself and to others around me. I imagine how good that feels. I am happy to be able to sense how good that feels.

Now let's focus on my ideal outcome which is [Add Title of Session].   I breathe deeply and fully and know that as I do, I am welcoming the happy reality I seek. [Add Affirmation Here] I imagine that every breath I take brings more and more goodness into my life. Every breath I release removes what I no longer want in my life, easily and effortlessly. I am becoming lighter and lighter as I release tensions, past disappointments, and old sorrows. These emotions and feelings no longer serve me. Releasing these feelings leaves so much more space for the good that awaits me. [Add Affirmation Here]

As I read this Hypnotic Narrative, I am aware that the words I see on this page are creating energy forms that are being created just for me.   I feel my eyelids getting heavy as the power of these moments of creation becomes more real to me.   I feel a warm, dreamy relaxation moving through my body as my eyes take in these words. I feel it now. And I know that this feeling brings with it the growing likelihood of my ideal outcome finding me. [Affirmation Here]

As I continue to breathe deeply, I imagine myself moving or floating down a set of stairs. As I float down the stairs, I become more and more relaxed. I realize that I can reach a hypnotic state with my eyes open, even though it's becoming harder and harder to keep my eyes open as I become more and more relaxed. [Affirmation Here]

As I continue to breathe deeply, I feel all cares and worries leave my body. I feel at peace and at ease, at one with the Universe and with my central goal. If I were to close my eyes for a moment, I would feel my energy coalescing with my ideal outcome. As my goal and I become one, the outer reality of that goal comes closer to fruition. [Affirmation Here]

I can feel my body relaxing more and more. [Affirmation Here] I realize that becoming or attracting whatever I want, is as easy as relaxing, opening myself to that possibility, and allowing that reality into my world. [Affirmation Here] This new reality can feel a bit odd, new, and good all at the same time I allow myself to sense the twinkle of happiness I feel about this ideal outcome. I allow myself to anticipate the pleasure that comes to myself and others as I reach my goal. I know that struggle is pointless and so unnecessary once I truly decide what I want, and simply invite the reality of [Affirmation Here] into my life.

I truly look forward to improved health and improved relationships, now that I realize that struggle is needless and counter-productive to reaching my goal of [Title of Affirmation]. As I continue to allow myself to feel how good this new reality is for me, I commit to using my EOSH sessions daily to give this new reality even more life force.

As I continue to breathe deeply, I feel myself expanding energetically, breathing freely, releasing any remaining old tensions, and moving closer and closer to achieving my ideal outcome. [Affirmation Here]

As I continue to allow myself to become one with my goal, I have a sense of peace that seems to erase any worries or fears I may have had awhile ago. I feel as if I've created a safe space in which to focus on achieving my goal without struggle or strife. I want this feeling of peace and inner quiet to stay with me throughout the day and decide to reinforce this wonderful feeling whenever I can today. I am looking forward to refocusing on my goals again and again throughout the day.

I am grateful to be able to enlist my inner genius to help me to achieve my goal. [Affirmation Here] I am happy and confident that achieving my goal is right around the corner. I am certain that at my moment of perfect readiness, my goal will be achieved.

As I look around, I remember where I am. I smile to realize how deeply involved I've become in my EOSH Primary Hypnotic Narrative. My body feels relaxed; I have a sense of otherworldliness, sort of out of space and time. I feel good. I am happy to be alive, happy to be here and happy to be me. I am grateful for this experience and look forward to the next time.

I realize it's time to return to my outer reality. As I take a final deep and cleansing breath, I feel my attention and focus returning to the world around me. It's time to be back to reality and it's good to be back. I will keep watch today for all of the goodness that's headed my way.

READY TO USE EOSH PRIMARY SESSIONS

These sessions are listed alphabetically for your ease of use within each category. Choose one Primary Session and use it daily for a month or so along with the matching Bonus Session found in Chapter 5. If you miss a day here or there, don't be concerned. Your mind is creating new belief patterns as you use these sessions. Daily use is ideal, but sticking with the program until your desired changes occur, is the primary objective.

PRIMARY EOSH SESSIONS

CAREER SESSIONS

BALANCING WORK & HOME

Breathing deeply, I relax my shoulders, my jaw, and the corners of my mouth. My hands feel pleasantly heavy and I lay them on my knees. I can feel how heavy they seem. I breathe deeply and imagine my life as a canvas on which I will be painting today. I can imagine painting the beautiful picture that my life can be.

I believe that I am empowered to create miracles in my life. As I accept this, that reality awakens and begins to form as part of my belief system. I imagine how good it feels to be a magnet for all good things, all good events and all good people. I allow myself to sense how happy I am becoming, as a person whose energy attracts all goodness to myself and others around me. I imagine how good that feels. I am happy to be able to sense how good that feels.

Now let's focus on my ideal outcome which is balancing work & home. I breathe deeply and fully and know that as I do, I am welcoming the happy reality I seek. I enjoy being at home and I enjoy being at work. I imagine that every breath I take brings more and more goodness into my life. Every breath I release removes what I no longer want in my life, easily and effortlessly. I am becoming lighter and lighter as I release tensions, past disappointments, and old sorrows. These emotions and feelings no longer serve me. Releasing these feelings leaves so much more space for the good that awaits me. I balance my time and attention between work and home.

As I read this Hypnotic Narrative, I am aware that the words I see on this page are creating energy forms that are being created just for me. I feel my eyelids getting heavy as the power of these moments of creation becomes more real to me. I feel a warm, dreamy relaxation moving through my body as my eyes take in these words. I feel it now. And I know that this feeling brings with it the growing likelihood of my ideal outcome finding me. I am always mentally at home when I am physically at home.

As I continue to breathe deeply, I imagine myself moving or floating down a set of stairs. As I float down the stairs, I become more and more relaxed. I realize that I can reach an hypnotic state with my eyes open, even though it's becoming harder and harder to keep my eyes open as I become more and more relaxed. I look forward to going home at the end of the day. I also look forward to returning to work when it's time.

As I continue to breathe deeply, I feel all cares and worries leave my body. I feel at peace and at ease, at one with the Universe and with my central goal. If I were to close my eyes for a moment, I could feel my energy coalescing with my ideal outcome. As my goal and I become one, the outer reality of that goal comes closer to fruition. I always balance both home and work.

58

I can feel my body relaxing more and more. I love being at home and I love being at work. I realize that becoming or attracting whatever I want, is as easy as relaxing, opening myself to that possibility, and allowing that reality into my world. I balance my time and attention between work and home. This new reality can feel a bit odd, new, and good all at the same time   I allow myself to sense the twinkle of happiness I feel about this ideal outcome. I allow myself to anticipate the pleasure that comes to myself and others as I reach my goal. I know that struggle is pointless and so unnecessary once I truly decide what I want, and simply invite the reality of balancing work and home into my life.

I truly look forward to improved health and improved relationships, now that I realize that struggle is needless and counter-productive to reaching my goal of balance. As I continue to allow myself to feel how good this new reality is for me, I commit to using my EOSH sessions daily to give this new reality even more life.

As I continue to breathe deeply, I feel myself expanding energetically, breathing freely, releasing any remaining old tensions, and moving closer and closer to achieving my ideal outcome. It's easy to balance my time between work and home.

As I continue to allow myself to become one with my goal, I have a sense of peace that seems to erase any worries or fears I may have had awhile ago. I feel as if I've created a safe space in which to focus on achieving my goal without struggle or strife. I want this feeling of peace and inner quiet to stay with me throughout the day and decide to reinforce this wonderful feeling whenever you can today. I am looking forward to refocusing on my goals again and again throughout the day.

I am grateful to be able to enlist my inner genius to help me to achieve my goal. I am always mentally at home when I am physically at home. I am happy and confident that achieving my goal is right around the corner. I am certain that at my moment of perfect readiness, my goal will be achieved.

As I look around, I remember where I am. I smile to realize how deeply involved I've become in my EOSH Primary Hypnotic Narrative. My body feels relaxed; I have a sense of otherworldliness, sort of out of space and time. I feel good. I am happy to be alive and happy to be here and happy to be me. I am grateful for this experience and look forward to the next time.

I realize it's time to return to my outer reality. As I take a final deep and cleansing breath, I feel my attention and focus returning to the world around me. It's time to be back to reality and it's good to be back. I will keep watch today for all of the goodness that's headed my way.

BRINGING MY "A" GAME CONSISTENTLY

Breathing deeply, I relax my shoulders, my jaw, and the corners of my mouth. My hands feel pleasantly heavy and I lay them on my knees. I can feel how heavy they seem. I breathe deeply and imagine my life as a canvas on which I will be painting today. I can imagine painting the beautiful picture that my life can be.

I believe that I am empowered to create miracles in my life. As I accept this, that reality awakens and begins to form as part of my belief system. I imagine how good it feels to be a magnet for all good things, all good events and all good people. I allow myself to sense how happy I am becoming, as a person whose energy attracts all goodness to myself and others around me. I imagine how good that feels. I am happy to be able to sense how good that feels.

Now let's focus on my ideal outcome which is bringing my "A" game consistently. I breathe deeply and fully and know that as I do, I am welcoming the happy reality I seek. I love to work I imagine that every breath I take brings more and more goodness into my life. Every breath I release removes what I no longer want in my life, easily and effortlessly. I am becoming lighter and lighter as I release tensions, past disappointments, and old sorrows. These emotions and feelings no longer serve me. Releasing these feelings leaves so much more space for the good that awaits me. I love to do my best.

As I read this Hypnotic Narrative, I am aware that the words I see on this page are creating energy forms that are being created just for me. I feel my eyelids getting heavy as the power of these moments of creation becomes more real to me. I feel a warm, dreamy relaxation moving through my body as my eyes take in these words. I feel it now. And I know that this feeling brings with it the growing likelihood of my ideal outcome finding me. My self esteem is based in part on my doing a good job.

As I continue to breathe deeply, I imagine myself moving or floating down a set of stairs. As I float down the stairs, I become more and more relaxed. I realize that I can reach an hypnotic state with my eyes open, even though it's becoming harder and harder to keep my eyes open as I become more and more relaxed. As I do my best, I profit myself and others.

As I continue to breathe deeply, I feel all cares and worries leave my body. I feel at peace and at ease, at one with the Universe and with my central goal. If I were to close my eyes for a moment, I could feel my energy coalescing with my ideal outcome. As my goal and I become one, the outer reality of that goal comes closer to fruition. Setting the bar high makes me a more valuable employee.

I can feel my body relaxing more and more. I respect those who perform their jobs professionally. I realize that becoming or attracting whatever I want, is as easy as relaxing, opening myself to that possibility, and allowing that reality into my world. This new reality can feel a bit odd, new, and good all at the same time I allow myself to sense the twinkle of happiness I feel about this ideal outcome. I allow myself to anticipate the pleasure that comes to myself and others as I reach my goal. I know that struggle is pointless and so unnecessary once I truly decide what I want, and simply invite the reality of bringing my "A" consistently into my life.

I truly look forward to improved health and improved relationships, now that I realize that struggle is needless and counter-productive to reaching my goal of bringing my "A" game at work. As I continue to allow myself to feel how good this new reality is for me, I commit to using my EOSH sessions daily to give this new reality even more life.

As I continue to breathe deeply, I feel myself expanding energetically, breathing freely, releasing any remaining old tensions, and moving closer and closer to achieving my ideal outcome. I respect those who perform their jobs professionally. I enjoy being considered one of those people.

As I continue to allow myself to become one with my goal, I have a sense of peace that seems to erase any worries or fears I may have had awhile ago. I feel as if I've created a safe space in which to focus on achieving my goal without struggle or strife. I want this feeling of peace and inner quiet to stay with me throughout the day and decide to reinforce this wonderful feeling whenever you can today. I am looking forward to refocusing on my goals again and again throughout the day.

I am grateful to be able to enlist my inner genius to help me to achieve my goal. I love to do my best. I am happy and confident that achieving my goal is right around the corner. I am certain that at my moment of perfect readiness, my goal will be achieved.

As I look around, I remember where I am. I smile to realize how deeply involved I've become in my EOSH Primary Hypnotic Narrative. My body feels relaxed; I have a sense of otherworldliness, sort of out of space and time. I feel good. I am happy to be alive and happy to be here and happy to be me. I am grateful for this experience and look forward to the next time.

I realize it's time to return to my outer reality. As I take a final deep and cleansing breath, I feel my attention and focus returning to the world around me. It's time to be back to reality and it's good to be back. I will keep watch today for all of the goodness that's headed my way.

BUSINESS PROSPERITY

Breathing deeply, I relax my shoulders, my jaw, and the corners of my mouth. My hands feel pleasantly heavy and I lay them on my knees. I can feel how heavy they seem. I breathe deeply and imagine my life as a canvas on which I will be painting today. I can imagine painting the beautiful picture that my life can be.

I believe that I am empowered to create miracles in my life. As I accept this, that reality awakens and begins to form as part of my belief system. I imagine how good it feels to be a magnet for all good things, all good events and all good people. I allow myself to sense how happy I am becoming, as a person whose energy attracts all goodness to myself and others around me. I imagine how good that feels. I am happy to be able to sense how good that feels.

Now let's focus on my ideal outcome which is business prosperity. I breathe deeply and fully and know that as I do, I am welcoming the happy reality I seek. My business is prosperous. I imagine that every breath I take brings more and more goodness into my life. Every breath I release removes what I no longer want in my life, easily and effortlessly. I am becoming lighter and lighter as I release tensions, past disappointments, and old sorrows. These emotions and feelings no longer serve me. Releasing these feelings leaves so much more space for the good that awaits me. Money comes easily to me and to my company.

As I read this Hypnotic Narrative, I am aware that the words I see on this page are creating energy forms that are being created just for me. I feel my eyelids getting heavy as the power of these moments of creation becomes more real to me. I feel a warm, dreamy relaxation moving through my body as my eyes take in these words. I feel it now. And I know that this feeling brings with it the growing likelihood of my ideal outcome finding me. I love knowing that there is an infinite supply of money and customers.

As I continue to breathe deeply, I imagine myself moving or floating down a set of stairs. As I float down the stairs, I become more and more relaxed. I realize that I can reach an hypnotic state with my

eyes open, even though it's becoming harder and harder to keep my eyes open as I become more and more relaxed. My business does better day by day.

As I continue to breathe deeply, I feel all cares and worries leave my body. I feel at peace and at ease, at one with the Universe and with my central goal. If I were to close my eyes for a moment, I could feel my energy coalescing with my ideal outcome. As my goal and I become one, the outer reality of that goal comes closer to fruition. I have complete faith in my business success.

I can feel my body relaxing more and more. I am sure that my customers are happy because that's one of my priorities. I realize that becoming or attracting whatever I want, is as easy as relaxing, opening myself to that possibility, and allowing that reality into my world. I have complete faith in my business success. This new reality can feel a bit odd, new, and good all at the same time I allow myself to sense the twinkle of happiness I feel about this ideal outcome. I allow myself to anticipate the pleasure that comes to myself and others as I reach my goal. I know that struggle is pointless and so unnecessary once I truly decide what I want, and simply invite the reality of business prosperity into my life.

I truly look forward to improved health and improved relationships, now that I realize that struggle is needless and counter-productive to reaching my goal of Business Prosperity. As I continue to allow myself to feel how good this new reality is for me, I commit to using my EOSH sessions daily to give this new reality even more life.

As I continue to breathe deeply, I feel myself expanding energetically, breathing freely, releasing any remaining old tensions, and moving closer and closer to achieving my ideal outcome. My business does better day by day.

As I continue to allow myself to become one with my goal, I have a sense of peace that seems to erase any worries or fears I may have had awhile ago. I feel as if I've created a safe space in which to focus on achieving my goal without struggle or strife. I want this feeling of peace and inner quiet to stay with me throughout the day and decide to reinforce this wonderful feeling whenever you can today. I am looking forward to refocusing on my goals again and again throughout the day.

I am grateful to be able to enlist my inner genius to help me to achieve my goal. My business is prosperous. I am happy and confident that achieving my goal is right around the corner. I am certain that at my moment of perfect readiness, my goal will be achieved.

As I look around, I remember where I am. I smile to realize how deeply involved I've become in my EOSH Primary Hypnotic Narrative. My body feels relaxed; I have a sense of otherworldliness, sort of out of space and time. I feel good. I am happy to be alive and happy to be here and happy to be me. I am grateful for this experience and look forward to the next time.

I realize it's time to return to my outer reality. As I take a final deep and cleansing breath, I feel my attention and focus returning to the world around me. It's time to be back to reality and it's good to be

back. I will keep watch today for all of the goodness that's headed my way.

CONFIDENCE AT WORK

Breathing deeply, I relax my shoulders, my jaw, and the corners of my mouth. My hands feel pleasantly heavy and I lay them on my knees. I can feel how heavy they seem. I breathe deeply and imagine my life as a canvas on which I will be painting today. I can imagine painting the beautiful picture that my life can be.

I believe that I am empowered to create miracles in my life. As I accept this, that reality awakens and begins to form as part of my belief system. I imagine how good it feels to be a magnet for all good things, all good events and all good people. I allow myself to sense how happy I am becoming, as a person whose energy attracts all goodness to myself and others around me. I imagine how good that feels. I am happy to be able to sense how good that feels.

Now let's focus on my ideal outcome which is confidence at work. I breathe deeply and fully and know that as I do, I am welcoming the happy reality I seek. I am confident in my ability to do my job. I imagine that every breath I take brings more and more goodness into my life. Every breath I release removes what I no longer want in my life, easily and effortlessly. I am becoming lighter and lighter as I release tensions, past disappointments, and old sorrows. These emotions and feelings no longer serve me. Releasing these feelings leaves so much more space for the good that awaits me. I know that I am a person who gives 100% to his job.

As I read this Hypnotic Narrative, I am aware that the words I see on this page are creating energy forms that are being created just for me. I feel my eyelids getting heavy as the power of these moments of creation becomes more real to me. I feel a warm, dreamy relaxation moving through my body as my eyes take in these words. I feel it now. And I know that this feeling brings with it the growing likelihood of my ideal outcome finding me. I am proud of the work that I do.

As I continue to breathe deeply, I imagine myself moving or floating down a set of stairs. As I float down the stairs, I become more and more relaxed. I realize that I can reach an hypnotic state with my eyes open, even though it's becoming harder and harder to keep my eyes open as I become more and more relaxed. I enjoy contributing to my company and to society.

As I continue to breathe deeply, I feel all cares and worries leave my body. I feel at peace and at ease, at one with the Universe and with my central goal. If I were to close my eyes for a moment, I could feel my energy coalescing with my ideal outcome. As my goal and I become one, the outer reality of that goal comes closer to fruition. I know that I am highly regarded at my company.

I can feel my body relaxing more and more. I am confident in my ability to do my job well. I realize that becoming or attracting whatever I want, is as easy as relaxing, opening myself to that possibility, and allowing that reality into my world. I know that I give 100% to my job. This new reality can feel a bit odd, new, and good all at the same time. I allow myself to sense the twinkle of happiness I feel about this ideal outcome. I allow myself to anticipate the pleasure that comes to myself and others as I reach my goal. I know that struggle is pointless and so unnecessary once I truly decide what I want, and simply invite the reality of more Confidence at Work into my life.

I truly look forward to improved health and improved relationships, now that I realize that struggle is needless and counter-productive to reaching my goal of confidence at work. As I continue to allow myself to feel how good this new reality is for me, I commit to using my EOSH sessions daily to give this new reality even more life.

As I continue to breathe deeply, I feel myself expanding energetically, breathing freely, releasing any remaining old tensions, and moving closer and closer to achieving my ideal outcome. I enjoy being praised for doing great work.

As I continue to allow myself to become one with my goal, I have a sense of peace that seems to erase

any worries or fears I may have had awhile ago. I feel as if I've created a safe space in which to focus on achieving my goal without struggle or strife. I want this feeling of peace and inner quiet to stay with me throughout the day and decide to reinforce this wonderful feeling whenever you can today. I am looking forward to refocusing on my goals again and again throughout the day.

I am grateful to be able to enlist my inner genius to help me to achieve my goal. I am happy and confident that achieving my goal is right around the corner. I am certain that at my moment of perfect readiness, my goal will be achieved.

As I look around, I remember where I am. I smile to realize how deeply involved I've become in my EOSH Primary Hypnotic Narrative. My body feels relaxed; I have a sense of otherworldliness, sort of out of space and time. I feel good. I am happy to be alive and happy to be here and happy to be me. I am grateful for this experience and look forward to the next time.

I realize it's time to return to my outer reality. As I take a final deep and cleansing breath, I feel my attention and focus returning to the world around me. It's time to be back to reality and it's good to be back. I will keep watch today for all of the goodness that's headed my way.

DEALING WITH CONFLICT

Breathing deeply, I relax my shoulders, my jaw, and the corners of my mouth. My hands feel pleasantly heavy and I lay them on my knees. I can feel how heavy they seem. I breathe deeply and imagine my life as a canvas on which I will be painting today. I can imagine painting the beautiful picture that my life can be.

I believe that I am empowered to create miracles in my life. As I accept this, that reality awakens and begins to form as part of my belief system. I imagine how good it feels to be a magnet for all good things, all good events and all good people. I allow myself to sense how happy I am becoming, as a person whose energy attracts all goodness to myself and

77

others around me. I imagine how good that feels. I am happy to be able to sense how good that feels.

Now let's focus on my ideal outcome which is dealing well with conflict. I breathe deeply and fully and know that as I do, I am welcoming the happy reality I seek. I am a fair person. I imagine that every breath I take brings more and more goodness into my life. Every breath I release removes what I no longer want in my life, easily and effortlessly. I am becoming lighter and lighter as I release tensions, past disappointments, and old sorrows. These emotions and feelings no longer serve me. Releasing these feelings leaves so much more space for the good that awaits me. I am fair to everyone I deal with.

As I read this Hypnotic Narrative, I am aware that the words I see on this page are creating energy forms that are being created just for me. I feel my eyelids getting heavy as the power of these moments of creation becomes more real to me. I feel a warm, dreamy relaxation moving through my body as my eyes take in these words. I feel it now. And I know

that this feeling brings with it the growing likelihood of my ideal outcome finding me. I am easy to get along with and I avoid confrontation.

As I continue to breathe deeply, I imagine myself moving or floating down a set of stairs. As I float down the stairs, I become more and more relaxed. I realize that I can reach an hypnotic state with my eyes open, even though it's becoming harder and harder to keep my eyes open as I become more and more relaxed. When confrontation is unavoidable, I deal with it calmly. I never lose my temper because doing so is pointless.

As I continue to breathe deeply, I feel all cares and worries leave my body. I feel at peace and at ease, at one with the Universe and with my central goal. If I were to close my eyes for a moment, I could feel my energy coalescing with my ideal outcome. As my goal and I become one, the outer reality of that goal comes closer to fruition. In a conflict, the person who keeps his head and listens always wins.

I can feel my body relaxing more and more. I am a fair person and that makes me happy. I realize that becoming or attracting whatever I want, is as easy as relaxing, opening myself to that possibility, and allowing that reality into my world. I am fair to everyone I deal with. This new reality can feel a bit odd, new, and good all at the same time   I allow myself to sense the twinkle of happiness I feel about this ideal outcome.   I allow myself to anticipate the pleasure that comes to myself and others as I reach my goal. I know that struggle is pointless and so unnecessary once I truly decide what I want, and simply invite the reality of dealing well with conflict into my life.

I truly look forward to improved health and improved relationships, now that I realize that struggle is needless and counter-productive to reaching my goal of dealing well with conflict. As I continue to allow myself to feel how good this new reality is for me, I commit to using my EOSH sessions daily to give this new reality even more life.

As I continue to breathe deeply, I feel myself expanding energetically, breathing freely, releasing any remaining old tensions, and moving closer and closer to achieving my ideal outcome. I am easy to get along with and I avoid conflict.

As I continue to allow myself to become one with my goal, I have a sense of peace that seems to erase any worries or fears I may have had awhile ago. I feel as if I've created a safe space in which to focus on achieving my goal without struggle or strife. I want this feeling of peace and inner quiet to stay with me throughout the day and decide to reinforce this wonderful feeling whenever you can today. I am looking forward to refocusing on my goals again and again throughout the day.

I am grateful to be able to enlist my inner genius to help me to achieve my goal. When confrontation is unavoidable, I deal with it calmly and fairly. I am happy and confident that achieving my goal is right around the corner. I am certain that at my moment of perfect readiness, my goal will be achieved.

As I look around, I remember where I am. I smile to realize how deeply involved I've become in my EOSH Primary Hypnotic Narrative. My body feels relaxed; I have a sense of otherworldliness, sort of

out of space and time. I feel good. I am happy to be alive and happy to be here and happy to be me. I am grateful for this experience and look forward to the next time.

I realize it's time to return to my outer reality. As I take a final deep and cleansing breath, I feel my attention and focus returning to the world around me. It's time to be back to reality and it's good to be back. I will keep watch today for all of the goodness that's headed my way.

RELATIONSHIP SESSIONS

ATTRACTING THE PERFECT MATE

Breathing deeply, I relax my shoulders, my jaw, and the corners of my mouth. My hands feel pleasantly heavy and I lay them on my knees. I can feel how heavy they seem. I breathe deeply and imagine my life as a canvas on which I will be painting today. I can imagine painting the beautiful picture that my life can be.

I believe that I am empowered to create miracles in my life. As I accept this, that reality awakens and begins to form as part of my belief system. I imagine how good it feels to be a magnet for all good things, all good events and all good people. I allow myself to sense how happy I am becoming, as a person whose energy attracts all goodness to myself and others around me. I imagine how good that feels. I am happy to be able to sense how good that feels.

Now let's focus on my ideal outcome which is attracting the perfect mate. I breathe deeply and fully and know that as I do, I am welcoming the happy reality I seek. I am open to opportunities to connect with my mate. I imagine that every breath I take brings more and more goodness into my life. Every breath I release removes what I no longer want in my life, easily and effortlessly. I am becoming lighter and lighter as I release tensions, past disappointments, and old sorrows. These emotions and feelings no longer serve me. Releasing these feelings leaves so much more space for the good that awaits me. I picture the perfect meeting with him/her.

As I read this Hypnotic Narrative, I am aware that the words I see on this page are creating energy forms that are being created just for me. I feel my eyelids getting heavy as the power of these moments of creation becomes more real to me. I feel a warm, dreamy relaxation moving through my body as my eyes take in these words. I feel it now. And I know that this feeling brings with it the growing likelihood of my ideal outcome finding me. I deserve the perfect mate and invite him/her into my life.

As I continue to breathe deeply, I imagine myself moving or floating down a set of stairs. As I float down the stairs, I become more and more relaxed. I realize that I can reach an hypnotic state with my eyes open, even though it's becoming harder and harder to keep my eyes open as I become more and more relaxed. I invite the Universe to send him/her to me.

As I continue to breathe deeply, I feel all cares and worries leave my body. I feel at peace and at ease, at one with the Universe and with my central goal. If I were to close my eyes for a moment, I could feel my energy coalescing with my ideal outcome. As my goal and I become one, the outer reality of that goal comes closer to fruition. There is room in my heart for my mate.

I can feel my body relaxing more and more. My perfect mate is out there looking for me. I realize that becoming or attracting whatever I want, is as easy as relaxing, opening myself to that possibility, and allowing that reality into my world. I can picture the perfect meeting with him/her. This new reality

can feel a bit odd, new, and good all at the same time   I allow myself to sense the twinkle of happiness I feel about this ideal outcome. I allow myself to anticipate the pleasure that comes to myself and others as I reach my goal. I know that struggle is pointless and so unnecessary once I truly decide what I want, and simply invite the reality of attracting the per
fect mate into my life.

I truly look forward to improved health and improved relationships, now that I realize that struggle is needless and counter-productive to reaching my goal of attracting the perfect mate. As I continue to allow myself to feel how good this new reality is for me, I commit to using my EOSH sessions daily to give this new reality even more life.

As I continue to breathe deeply, I feel myself expanding energetically, breathing freely, releasing any remaining old tensions, and moving closer and closer to achieving my ideal outcome. I know that I deserve the perfect mate.

As I continue to allow myself to become one with my goal, I have a sense of peace that seems to erase

any worries or fears I may have had awhile ago. I feel as if I've created a safe space in which to focus on achieving my goal without struggle or strife. I want this feeling of peace and inner quiet to stay with me throughout the day and decide to reinforce this wonderful feeling whenever you can today. I am looking forward to refocusing on my goals again and again throughout the day.

I am grateful to be able to enlist my inner genius to help me to achieve my goal. I invite the Universe to send him/her to me. I am happy and confident that achieving my goal is right around the corner. I am certain that at my moment of perfect readiness, my goal will be achieved.

As I look around, I remember where I am. I smile to realize how deeply involved I've become in my EOSH Primary Hypnotic Narrative. My body feels relaxed; I have a sense of otherworldliness, sort of out of space and time. I feel good. I am happy to be alive and happy to be here and happy to be me. I am grateful for this experience and look forward to the next time.

I realize it's time to return to my outer reality. As I take a final deep and cleansing breath, I feel my attention and focus returning to the world around me. It's time to be back to reality and it's good to be back. I will keep watch today for all of the goodness that's headed my way.

DOORMAT NO MORE

Breathing deeply, I relax my shoulders, my jaw, and the corners of my mouth. My hands feel pleasantly heavy and I lay them on my knees. I can feel how heavy they seem. I breathe deeply and imagine my life as a canvas on which I will be painting today. I can imagine painting the beautiful picture that my life can be.

I believe that I am empowered to create miracles in my life. As I accept this, that reality awakens and begins to form as part of my belief system. I imagine how good it feels to be a magnet for all good things, all good events and all good people. I allow myself to sense how happy I am becoming, as a person whose energy attracts all goodness to myself and

others around me. I imagine how good that feels. I am happy to be able to sense how good that feels.

Now let's focus on my ideal outcome which is to no longer be a doormat. I breathe deeply and fully and know that as I do, I am welcoming the happy reality I seek. I am no longer willing to be treated disrespectfully. I imagine that every breath I take brings more and more goodness into my life. Every breath I release removes what I no longer want in my life, easily and effortlessly. I am becoming lighter and lighter as I release tensions, past disappointments, and old sorrows. These emotions and feelings no longer serve me. Releasing these feelings leaves so much more space for the good that awaits me. I treat others fairly at all times.

As I read this Hypnotic Narrative, I am aware that the words I see on this page are creating energy forms that are being created just for me. I feel my eyelids getting heavy as the power of these moments of creation becomes more real to me. I feel a warm, dreamy relaxation moving through my body as my eyes take in these words. I feel it now. And I know

that this feeling brings with it the growing likelihood of my ideal outcome finding me. I require others to treat me fairly and I treat them fairly in return.

As I continue to breathe deeply, I imagine myself moving or floating down a set of stairs. As I float down the stairs, I become more and more relaxed. I realize that I can reach an hypnotic state with my eyes open, even though it's becoming harder and harder to keep my eyes open as I become more and more relaxed. I am worthy of love and attention.

As I continue to breathe deeply, I feel all cares and worries leave my body. I feel at peace and at ease, at one with the Universe and with my central goal. If I were to close my eyes for a moment, I could feel my energy coalescing with my ideal outcome. As my goal and I become one, the outer reality of that goal comes closer to fruition. I am a person of value and appeal.

I can feel my body relaxing more and more. As long as I treat me kindly, others will too. I realize that becoming or attracting whatever I want, is as easy as relaxing, opening myself to that possibility, and allowing that reality into my world. I am no longer a doormat. This new reality can feel a bit odd, new, and good all at the same time. I allow myself to sense the twinkle of happiness I feel about this ideal outcome. I allow myself to anticipate the pleasure that comes to myself and others as I reach my goal. I know that struggle is pointless and so unnecessary once I truly decide what I want, and simply invite the reality of kind and loving attention into my life.

I truly look forward to improved health and improved relationships, now that I realize that struggle is needless and counter-productive to reaching my goal of being treated with kindness and respect. As I continue to allow myself to feel how good this new reality is for me, I commit to using my EOSH sessions daily to give this new reality even more life.

As I continue to breathe deeply, I feel myself expanding energetically, breathing freely, releasing any remaining old tensions, and moving closer and closer to achieving my ideal outcome. I am a person of value and appeal.

As I continue to allow myself to become one with my goal, I have a sense of peace that seems to erase any worries or fears I may have had awhile ago. I feel as if I've created a safe space in which to focus on achieving my goal without struggle or strife. I want this feeling of peace and inner quiet to stay with me throughout the day and decide to reinforce this wonderful feeling whenever you can today. I am looking forward to refocusing on my goals again and again throughout the day.

I am grateful to be able to enlist my inner genius to help me to achieve my goal. As long as I treat me kindly, others will too. I am happy and confident that achieving my goal is right around the corner. I am certain that at my moment of perfect readiness, my goal will be achieved.

As I look around, I remember where I am. I smile to realize how deeply involved I've become in my EOSH Primary Hypnotic Narrative. My body feels relaxed; I have a sense of otherworldliness, sort of out of space and time. I feel good. I am happy to be alive and happy to be here and happy to be me. I am grateful for this experience and look forward to the next time.

I realize it's time to return to my outer reality. As I take a final deep and cleansing breath, I feel my attention and focus returning to the world around me. It's time to be back to reality and it's good to be back. I will keep watch today for all of the goodness that's headed my way.

GREAT SEX

Breathing deeply, I relax my shoulders, my jaw, and the corners of my mouth. My hands feel pleasantly heavy and I lay them on my knees. I can feel how heavy they seem. I breathe deeply and imagine my life as a canvas on which I will be painting today. I can imagine painting the beautiful picture that my life can be.

I believe that I am empowered to create miracles in my life. As I accept this, that reality awakens and begins to form as part of my belief system. I imagine how good it feels to be a magnet for all good things, all good events and all good people. I allow myself to sense how happy I am becoming, as a person whose energy attracts all goodness to myself and others around me. I imagine how good that feels. I am happy to be able to sense how good that feels.

Now let's focus on my ideal outcome which is great sex. I breathe deeply and fully and know that as I do, I am welcoming the happy reality I seek. I'm lucky to be an affectionate person. I imagine that every breath I take brings more and more goodness into my life. Every breath I release removes what I no longer want in my life, easily and effortlessly. I am becoming lighter and lighter as I release tensions, past disappointments, and old sorrows. These emotions and feelings no longer serve me. Releasing these feelings leaves so much more space for the good that awaits me. I love to express my feelings with my body.

As I read this Hypnotic Narrative, I am aware that the words I see on this page are creating energy forms that are being created just for me. I feel my eyelids getting heavy as the power of these moments

of creation becomes more real to me. I feel a warm, dreamy relaxation moving through my body as my eyes take in these words. I feel it now. And I know that this feeling brings with it the growing likelihood of my ideal outcome finding me. I love to touch and be touched.

As I continue to breathe deeply, I imagine myself moving or floating down a set of stairs. As I float down the stairs, I become more and more relaxed. I realize that I can reach an hypnotic state with my eyes open, even though it's becoming harder and harder to keep my eyes open as I become more and more relaxed. Making love is natural and healing.

As I continue to breathe deeply, I feel all cares and worries leave my body. I feel at peace and at ease, at one with the Universe and with my central goal. If I were to close my eyes for a moment, I could feel my energy coalescing with my ideal outcome. As my goal and I become one, the outer reality of that goal comes closer to fruition. My body is always responsive to my lover/partner.

I can feel my body relaxing more and more. Just the sight of my lover's body thrills me. I realize that becoming or attracting whatever I want, is as easy as relaxing, opening myself to that possibility, and allowing that reality into my world. I love to touch the one I love. This new reality can feel a bit odd, new, and good all at the same time. I allow myself to sense the twinkle of happiness I feel about this ideal outcome. I allow myself to anticipate the pleasure that comes to myself and others as I reach my goal. I know that struggle is pointless and so unnecessary once I truly decide what I want, and simply invite the reality of great sex into my life.

I truly look forward to improved health and improved relationships, now that I realize that struggle is needless and counter-productive to reaching my goal of having great sex. As I continue to allow myself to feel how good this new reality is for me, I commit to using my EOSH sessions daily to give this new reality even more life.

As I continue to breathe deeply, I feel myself expanding energetically, breathing freely, releasing

any remaining old tensions, and moving closer and closer to achieving my ideal outcome. Making love is natural and healing.

As I continue to allow myself to become one with my goal, I have a sense of peace that seems to erase any worries or fears I may have had awhile ago. I feel as if I've created a safe space in which to focus on achieving my goal without struggle or strife. I want this feeling of peace and inner quiet to stay with me throughout the day and decide to reinforce this wonderful feeling whenever you can today. I am looking forward to refocusing on my goals again and again throughout the day.

I am grateful to be able to enlist my inner genius to help me to achieve my goal. I'm lucky to be an affectionate person. I am happy and confident that achieving my goal is right around the corner. I am certain that at my moment of perfect readiness, my goal will be achieved.

As I look around, I remember where I am. I smile to realize how deeply involved I've become in my EOSH Primary Hypnotic Narrative. My body feels

relaxed; I have a sense of otherworldliness, sort of out of space and time. I feel good. I am happy to be alive and happy to be here and happy to be me. I am grateful for this experience and look forward to the next time.

I realize it's time to return to my outer reality. As I take a final deep and cleansing breath, I feel my attention and focus returning to the world around me. It's time to be back to reality and it's good to be back. I will keep watch today for all of the goodness that's headed my way.

HAPPY HOME

Breathing deeply, I relax my shoulders, my jaw, and the corners of my mouth. My hands feel pleasantly heavy and I lay them on my knees. I can feel how heavy they seem. I breathe deeply and imagine my life as a canvas on which I will be painting today. I can imagine painting the beautiful picture that my life can be.

I believe that I am empowered to create miracles in my life. As I accept this, that reality awakens and begins to form as part of my belief system. I imagine how good it feels to be a magnet for all good things, all good events and all good people. I allow myself to sense how happy I am becoming, as a person whose energy attracts all goodness to myself and others around me. I imagine how good that feels. I am happy to be able to sense how good that feels.

Now let's focus on my ideal outcome which is a happy home. I breathe deeply and fully and know that as I do, I am welcoming the happy reality I seek. I am lucky to be surrounded by love. I imagine that every breath I take brings more and more goodness into my life. Every breath I release removes what I no longer want in my life, easily and effortlessly. I am becoming lighter and lighter as I release tensions, past disappointments, and old sorrows. These emotions and feelings no longer serve me. Releasing these feelings leaves so much more space for the good that awaits me. I put my family first.

As I read this Hypnotic Narrative, I am aware that the words I see on this page are creating energy forms that are being created just for me. I feel my eyelids getting heavy as the power of these moments of creation becomes more real to me. I feel a warm, dreamy relaxation moving through my body as my eyes take in these words. I feel it now. And I know that this feeling brings with it the growing likelihood of my ideal outcome finding me. I put my kids and husband/wife first.

As I continue to breathe deeply, I imagine myself moving or floating down a set of stairs. As I float down the stairs, I become more and more relaxed. I realize that I can reach an hypnotic state with my eyes open, even though it's becoming harder and harder to keep my eyes open as I become more and more relaxed. My family knows how much they matter to me.

As I continue to breathe deeply, I feel all cares and worries leave my body. I feel at peace and at ease, at one with the Universe and with my central goal. If I were to close my eyes for a moment, I could feel my energy coalescing with my ideal outcome. As my goal and I become one, the outer reality of that goal comes closer to fruition. I always look forward to coming home.

I can feel my body relaxing more and more. I take care of those I love and they take care of me. I realize that becoming or attracting whatever I want, is as easy as relaxing, opening myself to that possibility, and allowing that reality into my world. I have a happy home filled with love. This new reality can feel a bit odd, new, and good all at the same time   I allow myself to sense the twinkle of happiness I feel about this ideal outcome. I allow myself to anticipate the pleasure that comes to myself and others as I reach my goal. I know that struggle is pointless and so unnecessary once I truly decide what I want, and simply invite the reality of a happy home into my life.

I truly look forward to improved health and improved relationships, now that I realize that struggle is needless and counter-productive to reaching my goal of having a happy home. As I

101

continue to allow myself to feel how good this new reality is for me, I commit to using my EOSH sessions daily to give this new reality even more life.

As I continue to breathe deeply, I feel myself expanding energetically, breathing freely, releasing any remaining old tensions, and moving closer and closer to achieving my ideal outcome. I am lucky to be surrounded by love.

As I continue to allow myself to become one with my goal, I have a sense of peace that seems to erase any worries or fears I may have had awhile ago. I feel as if I've created a safe space in which to focus on achieving my goal without struggle or strife. I want this feeling of peace and inner quiet to stay with me throughout the day and decide to reinforce this wonderful feeling whenever you can today. I am looking forward to refocusing on my goals again and again throughout the day.

I am grateful to be able to enlist my inner genius to help me to achieve my goal. I am happy and confident that achieving my goal is right around the corner. I am certain that at my moment of perfect readiness, my goal will be achieved.

As I look around, I remember where I am. I smile to realize how deeply involved I've become in my EOSH Primary Hypnotic Narrative. My body feels relaxed; I have a sense of otherworldliness, sort of out of space and time. I feel good. I am happy to be alive and happy to be here and happy to be me. I am grateful for this experience and look forward to the next time.

I realize it's time to return to my outer reality. As I take a final deep and cleansing breath, I feel my attention and focus returning to the world around me. It's time to be back to reality and it's good to be back. I will keep watch today for all of the goodness that's headed my way.

HAPPY KIDS

Breathing deeply, I relax my shoulders, my jaw, and the corners of my mouth. My hands feel pleasantly heavy and I lay them on my knees. I can feel how heavy they seem. I breathe deeply and imagine my life as a canvas on which I will be painting today. I can imagine painting the beautiful picture that my life can be.

I believe that I am empowered to create miracles in my life. As I accept this, that reality awakens and begins to form as part of my belief system. I imagine how good it feels to be a magnet for all good things, all good events and all good people. I allow myself to sense how happy I am becoming, as a person whose energy attracts all goodness to myself and others around me. I imagine how good that feels. I am happy to be able to sense how good that feels.

Now let's focus on my ideal outcome which is happy kids. I breathe deeply and fully and know that as I do, I am welcoming the happy reality I seek. My kids are smart, funny and beautiful. I imagine that every breath I take brings more and more goodness into my life. Every breath I release removes what I no longer want in my life, easily and effortlessly. I am becoming lighter and lighter as I release tensions, past disappointments, and old sorrows. These emotions and feelings no longer serve me. Releasing these feelings leaves so much more space for the good that awaits me. I am patient with my kids.

As I read this Hypnotic Narrative, I am aware that the words I see on this page are creating energy forms that are being created just for me. I feel my eyelids getting heavy as the power of these moments of creation becomes more real to me. I feel a warm, dreamy relaxation moving through my body as my eyes take in these words. I feel it now. And I know that this feeling brings with it the growing likelihood of my ideal outcome finding me. Sometimes my children are a handful, but I love them just as they are.

As I continue to breathe deeply, I imagine myself moving or floating down a set of stairs. As I float down the stairs, I become more and more relaxed. I realize that I can reach an hypnotic state with my eyes open, even though it's becoming harder and harder to keep my eyes open as I become more and more relaxed. I always show my kids how much I love them.

As I continue to breathe deeply, I feel all cares and worries leave my body. I feel at peace and at ease, at one with the Universe and with my central goal. If I were to close my eyes for a moment, I could feel my energy coalescing with my ideal outcome. As my goal and I become one, the outer reality of that goal comes closer to fruition. I am proud of my children.

I can feel my body relaxing more and more. I always remember to be patient with my kids. I realize that becoming or attracting whatever I want, is as easy as relaxing, opening myself to that possibility, and allowing that reality into my world. I respect my children's wishes whenever I can. This new reality can feel a bit odd, new, and good all at the same time I allow myself to sense the twinkle of happiness I feel about this ideal outcome. I allow myself to anticipate the pleasure that comes to myself and others as I reach my goal. I know that struggle is pointless and so unnecessary once I truly decide what I want, and simply invite the reality of happy kids into my life.

I truly look forward to improved health and improved relationships, now that I realize that struggle is needless and counter-productive to reaching my goal of having happy kids. As I continue to allow myself to feel how good this new reality is for me, I commit to using my EOSH sessions daily to give this new reality even more life.

As I continue to breathe deeply, I feel myself expanding energetically, breathing freely, releasing any remaining old tensions, and moving closer and closer to achieving my ideal outcome. I am proud of my children.

As I continue to allow myself to become one with my goal, I have a sense of peace that seems to erase any worries or fears I may have had awhile ago. I feel as if I've created a safe space in which to focus on achieving my goal without struggle or strife. I want this feeling of peace and inner quiet to stay with me throughout the day and decide to reinforce this wonderful feeling whenever you can today. I am looking forward to refocusing on my goals again and again throughout the day.

I am grateful to be able to enlist my inner genius to help me to achieve my goal. I am patient with my children. I am happy and confident that achieving my goal is right around the corner. I am certain that at my moment of perfect readiness, my goal will be achieved.

As I look around, I remember where I am. I smile to realize how deeply involved I've become in my EOSH Primary Hypnotic Narrative. My body feels relaxed; I have a sense of otherworldliness, sort of out of space and time. I feel good. I am happy to be alive and happy to be here and happy to be me. I am grateful for this experience and look forward to the next time.

I realize it's time to return to my outer reality. As I take a final deep and cleansing breath, I feel my attention and focus returning to the world around me. It's time to be back to reality and it's good to be back. I will keep watch today for all of the goodness that's headed my way.

IN-LAW SUCCESS

Breathing deeply, I relax my shoulders, my jaw, and the corners of my mouth. My hands feel pleasantly heavy and I lay them on my knees. I can feel how heavy they seem. I breathe deeply and imagine my life as a canvas on which I will be painting today. I can imagine painting the beautiful picture that my life can be.

I believe that I am empowered to create miracles in my life. As I accept this, that reality awakens and begins to form as part of my belief system. I imagine how good it feels to be a magnet for all good things, all good events and all good people. I allow myself to sense how happy I am becoming, as a person whose energy attracts all goodness to myself and others around me. I imagine how good that feels. I am happy to be able to sense how good that feels.

Now let's focus on my ideal outcome which is in-law success. I breathe deeply and fully and know that as I do, I am welcoming the happy reality I seek. My in-laws are family. I imagine that every breath I take brings more and more goodness into my life. Every breath I release removes what I no longer want in my life, easily and effortlessly. I am becoming lighter and lighter as I release tensions, past disappointments, and old sorrows. These emotions and feelings no longer serve me. Releasing these feelings leaves so much more space for the good that awaits me. My in-laws love my wife/husband and that's important.

As I read this Hypnotic Narrative, I am aware that the words I see on this page are creating energy forms that are being created just for me. I feel my eyelids getting heavy as the power of these moments of creation becomes more real to me. I feel a warm, dreamy relaxation moving through my body as my eyes take in these words. I feel it now. And I know that this feeling brings with it the growing likelihood of my ideal outcome finding me. My in-laws matter a lot to my spouse, so I get along with them just fine.

As I continue to breathe deeply, I imagine myself moving or floating down a set of stairs. As I float down the stairs, I become more and more relaxed. I realize that I can reach an hypnotic state with my

eyes open, even though it's becoming harder and harder to keep my eyes open as I become more and more relaxed. My in-laws are generous with our kids.

As I continue to breathe deeply, I feel all cares and worries leave my body. I feel at peace and at ease, at one with the Universe and with my central goal. If I were to close my eyes for a moment, I could feel my energy coalescing with my ideal outcome. As my goal and I become one, the outer reality of that goal comes closer to fruition. Seeing them is always a pleasure.

I can feel my body relaxing more and more. I like my in-laws very much. I realize that becoming or attracting whatever I want, is as easy as relaxing, opening myself to that possibility, and allowing that reality into my world. They are always kind to me. This new reality can feel a bit odd, new, and good all at the same time I allow myself to sense the twinkle of happiness I feel about this ideal outcome. I allow myself to anticipate the pleasure that comes to myself and others as I reach my goal. I know that struggle is pointless and so unnecessary once I truly decide what I want, and simply invite the reality of in-law success into my life.

I truly look forward to improved health and improved relationships, now that I realize that struggle is needless and counter-productive to reaching my goal of happy relations with the in-laws. As I continue to allow myself to feel how good this new reality is for me, I commit to using my EOSH sessions daily to give this new reality even more life.

As I continue to breathe deeply, I feel myself expanding energetically, breathing freely, releasing any remaining old tensions, and moving closer and closer to achieving my ideal outcome. My in-laws are family.

As I continue to allow myself to become one with my goal, I have a sense of peace that seems to erase any worries or fears I may have had awhile ago. I feel as if I've created a safe space in which to focus on achieving my goal without struggle or strife. I want this feeling of peace and inner quiet to stay with me throughout the day and decide to reinforce this wonderful feeling whenever you can today. I am looking forward to refocusing on my goals again and again throughout the day.

I am grateful to be able to enlist my inner genius to help me to achieve my goal. My in-laws love my wife/husband very much and that matters to me. I am happy and confident that achieving my goal is right around the corner. I am certain that at my moment of perfect readiness, my goal will be achieved.

As I look around, I remember where I am. I smile to realize how deeply involved I've become in my EOSH Primary Hypnotic Narrative. My body feels relaxed; I have a sense of otherworldliness, sort of out of space and time. I feel good. I am happy to be alive and happy to be here and happy to be me. I am grateful for this experience and look forward to the next time.

I realize it's time to return to my outer reality. As I take a final deep and cleansing breath, I feel my attention and focus returning to the world around me. It's time to be back to reality and it's good to be

back. I will keep watch today for all of the goodness that's headed my way.

MAKING FRIENDS EASILY

Breathing deeply, I relax my shoulders, my jaw, and the corners of my mouth. My hands feel pleasantly heavy and I lay them on my knees. I can feel how heavy they seem. I breathe deeply and imagine my life as a canvas on which I will be painting today. I can imagine painting the beautiful picture that my life can be.

I believe that I am empowered to create miracles in my life. As I accept this, that reality awakens and begins to form as part of my belief system. I imagine how good it feels to be a magnet for all good things, all good events and all good people. I allow myself to sense how happy I am becoming, as a person whose energy attracts all goodness to myself and others around me. I imagine how good that feels. I am happy to be able to sense how good that feels.

114

Now let's focus on my ideal outcome which is making friends easily. I breathe deeply and fully and know that as I do, I am welcoming the happy reality I seek. I love meeting new people and getting to know them. I imagine that every breath I take brings more and more goodness into my life. Every breath I release removes what I no longer want in my life, easily and effortlessly. I am becoming lighter and lighter as I release tensions, past disappointments, and old sorrows. These emotions and feelings no longer serve me. Releasing these feelings leaves so much more space for the good that awaits me. I never hesitate to say hello to someone new.

As I read this Hypnotic Narrative, I am aware that the words I see on this page are creating energy forms that are being created just for me. I feel my eyelids getting heavy as the power of these moments of creation becomes more real to me. I feel a warm, dreamy relaxation moving through my body as my eyes take in these words. I feel it now. And I know that this feeling brings with it the growing likelihood of my ideal outcome finding me. I enjoy expanding my world to include new people.

115

As I continue to breathe deeply, I imagine myself moving or floating down a set of stairs. As I float down the stairs, I become more and more relaxed. I realize that I can reach an hypnotic state with my eyes open, even though it's becoming harder and harder to keep my eyes open as I become more and more relaxed. People are fascinating and I love to hear their stories

As I continue to breathe deeply, I feel all cares and worries leave my body. I feel at peace and at ease, at one with the Universe and with my central goal. If I were to close my eyes for a moment, I could feel my energy coalescing with my ideal outcome. As my goal and I become one, the outer reality of that goal comes closer to fruition. I really like people and people like me.

I can feel my body relaxing more and more. I take every opportunity to meet new people. I realize that becoming or attracting whatever I want, is as easy as relaxing, opening myself to that possibility, and allowing that reality into my world. I make new friends easily. This new reality can feel a bit odd, new, and good all at the same time. I allow myself to sense the twinkle of happiness I feel about this ideal outcome. I allow myself to anticipate the pleasure that comes to others and myself as I reach my goal. I know that struggle is pointless and so unnecessary once I truly decide what I want, and simply invite the reality of making friends easily into my life.

I truly look forward to improved health and improved relationships, now that I realize that struggle is needless and counter-productive to reaching my goal of making new friends easily. As I continue to allow myself to feel how good this new reality is for me, I commit to using my EOSH sessions daily to give this new reality even more life.

As I continue to breathe deeply, I feel myself expanding energetically, breathing freely, releasing any remaining old tensions, and moving closer and closer to achieving my ideal outcome. I love meeting new people and getting to know them.

As I continue to allow myself to become one with my goal, I have a sense of peace that seems to erase any worries or fears I may have had awhile ago. I

117

feel as if I've created a safe space in which to focus on achieving my goal without struggle or strife. I want this feeling of peace and inner quiet to stay with me throughout the day and decide to reinforce this wonderful feeling whenever you can today. I am looking forward to refocusing on my goals again and again throughout the day.

I am grateful to be able to enlist my inner genius to help me to achieve my goal. I never hesitate to say hello to someone new. I am happy and confident that achieving my goal is right around the corner. I am certain that at my moment of perfect readiness, my goal will be achieved.

As I look around, I remember where I am. I smile to realize how deeply involved I've become in my EOSH Primary Hypnotic Narrative. My body feels relaxed; I have a sense of otherworldliness, sort of out of space and time. I feel good. I am happy to be alive and happy to be here and happy to be me. I am grateful for this experience and look forward to the next time.

I realize it's time to return to my outer reality. As I take a final deep and cleansing breath, I feel my attention and focus returning to the world around me. It's time to be back to reality and it's good to be back. I will keep watch today for all of the goodness that's headed my way.

PERSONAL PAMPERING

Breathing deeply, I relax my shoulders, my jaw, and the corners of my mouth. My hands feel pleasantly heavy and I lay them on my knees. I can feel how heavy they seem. I breathe deeply and imagine my life as a canvas on which I will be painting today. I can imagine painting the beautiful picture that my life can be.

I believe that I am empowered to create miracles in my life. As I accept this, that reality awakens and begins to form as part of my belief system. I imagine how good it feels to be a magnet for all good things, all good events and all good people. I allow myself to sense how happy I am becoming, as a person whose energy attracts all goodness to myself and

119

others around me. I imagine how good that feels. I am happy to be able to sense how good that feels.

Now let's focus on my ideal outcome which is more personal pampering. I breathe deeply and fully and know that as I do, I am welcoming the happy reality I seek. I love to be pampered. I imagine that every breath I take brings more and more goodness into my life. Every breath I release removes what I no longer want in my life, easily and effortlessly. I am becoming lighter and lighter as I release tensions, past disappointments, and old sorrows. These emotions and feelings no longer serve me. Releasing these feelings leaves so much more space for the good that awaits me. I take every opportunity to be pampered.

As I read this Hypnotic Narrative, I am aware that the words I see on this page are creating energy forms that are being created just for me. I feel my eyelids getting heavy as the power of these moments of creation becomes more real to me. I feel a warm, dreamy relaxation moving through my body as my eyes take in these words. I feel it now. And I know

that this feeling brings with it the growing likelihood of my ideal outcome finding me. I love to take care of my hair and my body.

As I continue to breathe deeply, I imagine myself moving or floating down a set of stairs. As I float down the stairs, I become more and more relaxed. I realize that I can reach an hypnotic state with my eyes open, even though it's becoming harder and harder to keep my eyes open as I become more and more relaxed. I love to shop for beautiful clothes.

As I continue to breathe deeply, I feel all cares and worries leave my body. I feel at peace and at ease, at one with the Universe and with my central goal. If I were to close my eyes for a moment, I could feel my energy coalescing with my ideal outcome. As my goal and I become one, the outer reality of that goal comes closer to fruition. I take time for pampering.

I can feel my body relaxing more and more. I enjoy dressing up and going out. I realize that becoming or attracting whatever I want, is as easy as relaxing, opening myself to that possibility, and allowing that reality into my world. I always let my spouse/partner pamper me. This new reality can feel a bit odd, new, and good all at the same time. I allow myself to sense the twinkle of happiness I feel about this ideal outcome. I allow myself to anticipate the pleasure that comes to myself and others as I reach my goal. I know that struggle is pointless and so unnecessary once I truly decide what I want, and simply invite the reality of personal pampering into my life.

I truly look forward to improved health and improved relationships, now that I realize that struggle is needless and counter-productive to reaching my goal of personal pampering. As I continue to allow myself to feel how good this new reality is for me, I commit to using my EOSH sessions daily to give this new reality even more life.

As I continue to breathe deeply, I feel myself expanding energetically, breathing freely, releasing any remaining old tensions, and moving closer and closer to achieving my ideal outcome. I take every opportunity to be pampered.

As I continue to allow myself to become one with my goal, I have a sense of peace that seems to erase

any worries or fears I may have had awhile ago. I feel as if I've created a safe space in which to focus on achieving my goal without struggle or strife. I want this feeling of peace and inner quiet to stay with me throughout the day and decide to reinforce this wonderful feeling whenever you can today. I am looking forward to refocusing on my goals again and again throughout the day.

I am grateful to be able to enlist my inner genius to help me to achieve my goal. I love to take time for pampering. I am happy and confident that achieving my goal is right around the corner. I am certain that at my moment of perfect readiness, my goal will be achieved.

As I look around, I remember where I am. I smile to realize how deeply involved I've become in my EOSH Primary Hypnotic Narrative. My body feels relaxed; I have a sense of otherworldliness, sort of out of space and time. I feel good. I am happy to be alive and happy to be here and happy to be me. I am grateful for this experience and look forward to the next time.

I realize it's time to return to my outer reality. As I take a final deep and cleansing breath, I feel my attention and focus returning to the world around me. It's time to be back to reality and it's good to be back. I will keep watch today for all of the goodness that's headed my way.

RESPECT & KINDNESS

Breathing deeply, I relax my shoulders, my jaw, and the corners of my mouth. My hands feel pleasantly heavy and I lay them on my knees. I can feel how heavy they seem. I breathe deeply and imagine my life as a canvas on which I will be painting today. I can imagine painting the beautiful picture that my life can be.

I believe that I am empowered to create miracles in my life. As I accept this, that reality awakens and begins to form as part of my belief system. I imagine how good it feels to be a magnet for all good things, all good events and all good people. I allow myself to sense how happy I am becoming, as a person whose energy attracts all goodness to myself and

others around me. I imagine how good that feels. I am happy to be able to sense how good that feels.

Now let's focus on my ideal outcome which is respect and kindness. I breathe deeply and fully and know that as I do, I am welcoming the happy reality I seek. I deserve respect and kindness. I imagine that every breath I take brings more and more goodness into my life. Every breath I release removes what I no longer want in my life, easily and effortlessly. I am becoming lighter and lighter as I release tensions, past disappointments, and old sorrows. These emotions and feelings no longer serve me. Releasing these feelings leaves so much more space for the good that awaits me. I offer respect and kindness to everyone I encounter.

As I read this Hypnotic Narrative, I am aware that the words I see on this page are creating energy forms that are being created just for me. I feel my eyelids getting heavy as the power of these moments of creation becomes more real to me. I feel a warm, dreamy relaxation moving through my body as my eyes take in these words. I feel it now. And I know

that this feeling brings with it the growing likelihood of my ideal outcome finding me. I respect the rights of others.

As I continue to breathe deeply, I imagine myself moving or floating down a set of stairs. As I float down the stairs, I become more and more relaxed. I realize that I can reach an hypnotic state with my eyes open, even though it's becoming harder and harder to keep my eyes open as I become more and more relaxed. I respect the rights of others to hold opinions that differ from mine.

As I continue to breathe deeply, I feel all cares and worries leave my body. I feel at peace and at ease, at one with the Universe and with my central goal. If I were to close my eyes for a moment, I could feel my energy coalescing with my ideal outcome. As my goal and I become one, the outer reality of that goal comes closer to fruition. I listen to the opinions of others courteously.

I can feel my body relaxing more and more. I am intentionally kind to everyone. I realize that becoming or attracting whatever I want, is as easy as relaxing, opening myself to that possibility, and allowing that reality into my world. As I give respect and kindness to others, I receive it as well. This new reality can feel a bit odd, new, and good all at the same time. I allow myself to sense the twinkle of happiness I feel about this ideal outcome. I allow myself to anticipate the pleasure that comes to others and myself as I reach my goal. I know that struggle is pointless and so unnecessary once I truly decide what I want, and simply invite the reality of respect and kindness into my life.

I truly look forward to improved health and improved relationships, now that I realize that struggle is needless and counter-productive to reaching my goal of respect and kindness. As I continue to allow myself to feel how good this new reality is for me, I commit to using my EOSH sessions daily to give this new reality even more life.

As I continue to breathe deeply, I feel myself expanding energetically, breathing freely, releasing any remaining old tensions, and moving closer and closer to achieving my ideal outcome. I deserve respect and kindness.

As I continue to allow myself to become one with my goal, I have a sense of peace that seems to erase any worries or fears I may have had awhile ago. I feel as if I've created a safe space in which to focus on achieving my goal without struggle or strife. I want this feeling of peace and inner quiet to stay with me throughout the day and decide to reinforce this wonderful feeling whenever you can today. I am looking forward to refocusing on my goals again and again throughout the day.

I am grateful to be able to enlist my inner genius to help me to achieve my goal. I offer respect and kindness to everyone I encounter. I am happy and confident that achieving my goal is right around the corner. I am certain that at my moment of perfect readiness, my goal will be achieved.

As I look around, I remember where I am. I smile to realize how deeply involved I've become in my EOSH Primary Hypnotic Narrative. My body feels relaxed; I have a sense of otherworldliness, sort of

out of space and time. I feel good. I am happy to be alive and happy to be here and happy to be me. I am grateful for this experience and look forward to the next time.

I realize it's time to return to my outer reality. As I take a final deep and cleansing breath, I feel my attention and focus returning to the world around me. It's time to be back to reality and it's good to be back. I will keep watch today for all of the goodness that's headed my way.

SEEING THE GOOD IN OTHERS

Breathing deeply, I relax my shoulders, my jaw, and the corners of my mouth. My hands feel pleasantly heavy and I lay them on my knees. I can feel how heavy they seem. I breathe deeply and imagine my life as a canvas on which I will be painting today. I can imagine painting the beautiful picture that my life can be.

I believe that I am empowered to create miracles in my life. As I accept this, that reality awakens and begins to form as part of my belief system. I imagine how good it feels to be a magnet for all good things, all good events and all good people. I allow myself to sense how happy I am becoming, as a person whose energy attracts all goodness to myself and others around me. I imagine how good that feels. I am happy to be able to sense how good that feels.

Now let's focus on my ideal outcome which is seeing the good in others. I breathe deeply and fully and know that as I do, I am welcoming the happy reality I seek. I choose to see the best in others. I imagine that every breath I take brings more and more goodness into my life. Every breath I release removes what I no longer want in my life, easily and effortlessly. I am becoming lighter and lighter as I release tensions, past disappointments, and old sorrows. These emotions and feelings no longer serve me. Releasing these feelings leaves so much more space for the good that awaits me. I believe that most people are good.

As I read this Hypnotic Narrative, I am aware that the words I see on this page are creating energy forms that are being created just for me. I feel my eyelids getting heavy as the power of these moments of creation becomes more real to me. I feel a warm, dreamy relaxation moving through my body as my eyes take in these words. I feel it now. And I know that this feeling brings with it the growing likelihood of my ideal outcome finding me. I attract only good people into my life.

As I continue to breathe deeply, I imagine myself moving or floating down a set of stairs. As I float down the stairs, I become more and more relaxed. I realize that I can reach an hypnotic state with my eyes open, even though it's becoming harder and harder to keep my eyes open as I become more and more relaxed. I am happy to see a silver lining in every cloud.

As I continue to breathe deeply, I feel all cares and worries leave my body. I feel at peace and at ease, at one with the Universe and with my central goal. If I were to close my eyes for a moment, I could feel my energy coalescing with my ideal outcome. As my goal and I become one, the outer reality of that goal comes closer to fruition. I believe that everything happens for a reason.

I can feel my body relaxing more and more. I believe that as I am kind, so is the world. I realize that becoming or attracting whatever I want, is as easy as relaxing, opening myself to that possibility, and allowing that reality into my world. I choose to see the best in others. This new reality can feel a bit odd, new, and good all at the same time. I allow myself to sense the twinkle of happiness I feel about this ideal outcome. I allow myself to anticipate the pleasure that comes to others and myself as I reach my goal. I know that struggle is pointless and so unnecessary once I truly decide what I want, and simply invite the reality of seeing the best in others into my life.

I truly look forward to improved health and improved relationships, now that I realize that struggle is needless and counter-productive to reaching my goal of seeing the best in others. As I continue to allow myself to feel how good this new reality is for me, I commit to using my EOSH sessions daily to give this new reality even more life.

As I continue to breathe deeply, I feel myself expanding energetically, breathing freely, releasing any remaining old tensions, and moving closer and closer to achieving my ideal outcome. I am happy to see a silver lining in every cloud.

As I continue to allow myself to become one with my goal, I have a sense of peace that seems to erase any worries or fears I may have had awhile ago. I feel as if I've created a safe space in which to focus on achieving my goal without struggle or strife. I want this feeling of peace and inner quiet to stay with me throughout the day and decide to reinforce this wonderful feeling whenever you can today. I am looking forward to refocusing on my goals again and again throughout the day.

I am grateful to be able to enlist my inner genius to help me to achieve my goal. I only attract good people into my life. I am happy and confident that achieving my goal is right around the corner. I am certain that at my moment of perfect readiness, my goal will be achieved.

As I look around, I remember where I am. I smile to realize how deeply involved I've become in my EOSH Primary Hypnotic Narrative. My body feels relaxed; I have a sense of otherworldliness, sort of out of space and time. I feel good. I am happy to be alive and happy to be here and happy to be me. I am grateful for this experience and look forward to the next time.

I realize it's time to return to my outer reality. As I take a final deep and cleansing breath, I feel my attention and focus returning to the world around me. It's time to be back to reality and it's good to be back. I will keep watch today for all of the goodness that's headed my way.

SINGLE & LOVING IT

Breathing deeply, I relax my shoulders, my jaw, and the corners of my mouth. My hands feel pleasantly heavy and I lay them on my knees. I can feel how heavy they seem. I breathe deeply and imagine my life as a canvas on which I will be painting today. I can imagine painting the beautiful picture that my life can be.

I believe that I am empowered to create miracles in my life. As I accept this, that reality awakens and begins to form as part of my belief system. I imagine how good it feels to be a magnet for all good things, all good events and all good people. I allow myself to sense how happy I am becoming, as a person whose energy attracts all goodness to myself and others around me. I imagine how good that feels. I am happy to be able to sense how good that feels.

Now let's focus on my ideal outcome which is loving being single. I breathe deeply and fully and know that as I do, I am welcoming the happy reality I seek. Being single is good. I imagine that every breath I take brings more and more goodness into my life. Every breath I release removes what I no longer want in my life, easily and effortlessly. I am becoming lighter and lighter as I release tensions, past disappointments, and old sorrows. These emotions and feelings no longer serve me. Releasing these feelings leaves so much more space for the good that awaits me. Life as a single person is uncomplicated and simple.

As I read this Hypnotic Narrative, I am aware that the words I see on this page are creating energy forms that are being created just for me. I feel my eyelids getting heavy as the power of these moments of creation becomes more real to me. I feel a warm, dreamy relaxation moving through my body as my eyes take in these words. I feel it now. And I know that this feeling brings with it the growing likelihood of my ideal outcome finding me. There are no disagreements in a single household.

As I continue to breathe deeply, I imagine myself moving or floating down a set of stairs. As I float down the stairs, I become more and more relaxed. I realize that I can reach an hypnotic state with my eyes open, even though it's becoming harder and harder to keep my eyes open as I become more and more relaxed. The best thing about being single is that everything is still a possibility. A single person can meet the person of his/her dreams and act on it.

As I continue to breathe deeply, I feel all cares and worries leave my body. I feel at peace and at ease, at one with the Universe and with my central goal. If I were to close my eyes for a moment, I could feel my energy coalescing with my ideal outcome. As my goal and I become one, the outer reality of that goal comes closer to fruition. I love the freedom of being single.

I can feel my body relaxing more and more. I love not knowing what's around the next corner. I realize that becoming or attracting whatever I want, is as easy as relaxing, opening myself to that possibility, and allowing that reality into my world. Being single is good. This new reality can feel a bit odd, new, and good all at the same time. I allow myself to sense the twinkle of happiness I feel about this ideal outcome.

I allow myself to anticipate the pleasure that comes to myself and others as I reach my goal. I know that struggle is pointless and so unnecessary once I truly decide what I want, and simply invite the reality of loving being single into my life.

I truly look forward to improved health and improved relationships, now that I realize that struggle is needless and counter-productive to reaching my goal of loving being single. As I continue to allow myself to feel how good this new reality is for me, I commit to using my EOSH sessions daily to give this new reality even more life.

As I continue to breathe deeply, I feel myself expanding energetically, breathing freely, releasing any remaining old tensions, and moving closer and closer to achieving my ideal outcome. I love the freedom of being single.

As I continue to allow myself to become one with my goal, I have a sense of peace that seems to erase any worries or fears I may have had awhile ago. I feel as if I've created a safe space in which to focus on achieving my goal without struggle or strife. I want this feeling of peace and inner quiet to stay with me throughout the day and decide to reinforce this wonderful feeling whenever you can today. I am looking forward to refocusing on my goals again and again throughout the day.

I am grateful to be able to enlist my inner genius to help me to achieve my goal. Life is uncomplicated and simple when you're single. I am happy and confident that achieving my goal is right around the corner. I am certain that at my moment of perfect readiness, my goal will be achieved.

As I look around, I remember where I am. I smile to realize how deeply involved I've become in my EOSH Primary Hypnotic Narrative. My body feels relaxed; I have a sense of otherworldliness, sort of out of space and time. I feel good. I am happy to be alive and happy to be here and happy to be me. I am grateful for this experience and look forward to the next time.

I realize it's time to return to my outer reality. As I take a final deep and cleansing breath, I feel my attention and focus returning to the world around me. It's time to be back to reality and it's good to be back. I will keep watch today for all of the goodness that's headed my way.

STANDING YOUR GROUND

Breathing deeply, I relax my shoulders, my jaw, and the corners of my mouth. My hands feel pleasantly heavy and I lay them on my knees. I can feel how heavy they seem. I breathe deeply and imagine my life as a canvas on which I will be painting today. I can imagine painting the beautiful picture that my life can be.

I believe that I am empowered to create miracles in my life. As I accept this, that reality awakens and begins to form as part of my belief system. I imagine how good it feels to be a magnet for all good things, all good events and all good people. I allow myself to sense how happy I am becoming, as a person whose energy attracts all goodness to myself and others around me. I imagine how good that feels. I am happy to be able to sense how good that feels.

Now let's focus on my ideal outcome which is learning to stand my ground]. I breathe deeply and fully and know that as I do, I am welcoming the happy reality I seek. I can stand my ground peacefully. I imagine that every breath I take brings more and more goodness into my life. Every breath I release removes what I no longer want in my life, easily and effortlessly. I am becoming lighter and lighter as I release tensions, past disappointments, and old sorrows. These emotions and feelings no longer serve me. Releasing these feelings leaves so much more space for the good that awaits me. I am a strong, intelligent person capable of making my own decisions.

As I read this Hypnotic Narrative, I am aware that the words I see on this page are creating energy forms that are being created just for me. I feel my eyelids getting heavy as the power of these moments of creation becomes more real to me. I feel a warm, dreamy relaxation moving through my body as my eyes take in these words. I feel it now. And I know that this feeling brings with it the growing likelihood

of my ideal outcome finding me. I can assert myself pleasantly.

As I continue to breathe deeply, I imagine myself moving or floating down a set of stairs. As I float down the stairs, I become more and more relaxed. I realize that I can reach an hypnotic state with my eyes open, even though it's becoming harder and harder to keep my eyes open as I become more and more relaxed. I have control over my life.

As I continue to breathe deeply, I feel all cares and worries leave my body. I feel at peace and at ease, at one with the Universe and with my central goal. If I were to close my eyes for a moment, I could feel my energy coalescing with my ideal outcome. As my goal and I become one, the outer reality of that goal comes closer to fruition. I can win when I want to.

I can feel my body relaxing more and more. I am a strong, competent person. I realize that becoming or attracting whatever I want, is as easy as relaxing, opening myself to that possibility, and allowing that reality into my world. This new reality can feel a bit odd, new, and good all at the same time. I allow myself to sense the twinkle of happiness I feel about this ideal outcome. I allow myself to anticipate the pleasure that comes to myself and others as I reach my goal. I know that struggle is pointless and so unnecessary once I truly decide what I want, and simply invite the reality of standing my ground into my life.

I truly look forward to improved health and improved relationships, now that I realize that struggle is needless and counter-productive to reaching my goal of standing my ground. As I continue to allow myself to feel how good this new reality is for me, I commit to using my EOSH sessions daily to give this new reality even more life.

As I continue to breathe deeply, I feel myself expanding energetically, breathing freely, releasing any remaining old tensions, and moving closer and closer to achieving my ideal outcome. I can assert myself pleasantly.

As I continue to allow myself to become one with my goal, I have a sense of peace that seems to erase any worries or fears I may have had awhile ago. I

feel as if I've created a safe space in which to focus on achieving my goal without struggle or strife. I want this feeling of peace and inner quiet to stay with me throughout the day and decide to reinforce this wonderful feeling whenever you can today. I am looking forward to refocusing on my goals again and again throughout the day.

I am grateful to be able to enlist my inner genius to help me to achieve my goal. I can choose not to fight or disagree and still win. I am happy and confident that achieving my goal is right around the corner. I am certain that at my moment of perfect readiness, my goal will be achieved.

As I look around, I remember where I am. I smile to realize how deeply involved I've become in my EOSH Primary Hypnotic Narrative. My body feels relaxed; I have a sense of otherworldliness, sort of out of space and time. I feel good. I am happy to be alive and happy to be here and happy to be me. I am grateful for this experience and look forward to the next time.

I realize it's time to return to my outer reality. As I take a final deep and cleansing breath, I feel my attention and focus returning to the world around me. It's time to be back to reality and it's good to be back. I will keep watch today for all of the goodness that's headed my way.

GENERAL SESSIONS

ACCESSING MY HIGHER POWER

Breathing deeply, I relax my shoulders, my jaw, and the corners of my mouth. My hands feel pleasantly heavy and I lay them on my knees. I can feel how heavy they seem. I breathe deeply and imagine my life as a canvas on which I will be painting today. I can imagine painting the beautiful picture that my life can be.

I believe that I am empowered to create miracles in my life. As I accept this, that reality awakens and begins to form as part of my belief system. I imagine how good it feels to be a magnet for all good things, all good events and all good people. I allow myself

145

to sense how happy I am becoming, as a person whose energy attracts all goodness to myself and others around me. I imagine how good that feels. I am happy to be able to sense how good that feels.

Now let's focus on my ideal outcome which is accessing my higher power. I breathe deeply and fully and know that as I do, I am welcoming the happy reality I seek. I am always guided. I imagine that every breath I take brings more and more goodness into my life. Every breath I release removes what I no longer want in my life, easily and effortlessly. I am becoming lighter and lighter as I release tensions, past disappointments, and old sorrows. These emotions and feelings no longer serve me. Releasing these feelings leaves so much more space for the good that awaits me. I am protected.

As I read this Hypnotic Narrative, I am aware that the words I see on this page are creating energy forms that are being created just for me. I feel my eyelids getting heavy as the power of these moments of creation becomes more real to me. I feel a warm, dreamy relaxation moving through my body as my eyes take in these words. I feel it now. And I know that this feeling brings with it the growing likelihood of my ideal outcome finding me. I have access to group consciousness.

As I continue to breathe deeply, I imagine myself moving or floating down a set of stairs. As I float down the stairs, I become more and more relaxed. I realize that I can reach an hypnotic state with my eyes open, even though it's becoming harder and harder to keep my eyes open as I become more and more relaxed. I always receive the information I need.

As I continue to breathe deeply, I feel all cares and worries leave my body. I feel at peace and at ease, at one with the Universe and with my central goal. If I were to close my eyes for a moment, I could feel my energy coalescing with my ideal outcome. As my goal and I become one, the outer reality of that goal comes closer to fruition. I am connected to everything and everyone.

I can feel my body relaxing more and more. I am a light being. I realize that becoming or attracting whatever I want, is as easy as relaxing, opening myself to that possibility, and allowing that reality into my world. I am blessed. This new reality can feel a bit odd, new, and good all at the same time. I allow myself to sense the twinkle of happiness I feel about this ideal outcome. I allow myself to anticipate the pleasure that comes to myself and others as I reach my goal. I know that struggle is pointless and so unnecessary once I truly decide what I want, and simply invite the reality of accessing my higher power into my life.

I truly look forward to improved health and improved relationships, now that I realize that struggle is needless and counter-productive to reaching my goal of greater access to higher power. As I continue to allow myself to feel how good this new reality is for me, I commit to using my EOSH sessions daily to give this new reality even more life.

As I continue to breathe deeply, I feel myself expanding energetically, breathing freely, releasing

any remaining old tensions, and moving closer and closer to achieving my ideal outcome. I am always guided.

As I continue to allow myself to become one with my goal, I have a sense of peace that seems to erase any worries or fears I may have had awhile ago. I feel as if I've created a safe space in which to focus on achieving my goal without struggle or strife. I want this feeling of peace and inner quiet to stay with me throughout the day and decide to reinforce this wonderful feeling whenever you can today. I am looking forward to refocusing on my goals again and again throughout the day.

I am grateful to be able to enlist my inner genius to help me to achieve my goal. I am blessed. I am happy and confident that achieving my goal is right around the corner. I am certain that at my moment of perfect readiness, my goal will be achieved.

As I look around, I remember where I am. I smile to realize how deeply involved I've become in my EOSH Primary Hypnotic Narrative. My body feels relaxed; I have a sense of otherworldliness, sort of

149

out of space and time. I feel good. I am happy to be alive and happy to be here and happy to be me. I am grateful for this experience and look forward to the next time.

I realize it's time to return to my outer reality. As I take a final deep and cleansing breath, I feel my attention and focus returning to the world around me. It's time to be back to reality and it's good to be back. I will keep watch today for all of the goodness that's headed my way.

AGELESS

Breathing deeply, I relax my shoulders, my jaw, and the corners of my mouth. My hands feel pleasantly heavy and I lay them on my knees. I can feel how heavy they seem. I breathe deeply and imagine my life as a canvas on which I will be painting today. I can imagine painting the beautiful picture that my life can be.

I believe that I am empowered to create miracles in my life. As I accept this, that reality awakens and

150

begins to form as part of my belief system. I imagine how good it feels to be a magnet for all good things, all good events and all good people. I allow myself to sense how happy I am becoming, as a person whose energy attracts all goodness to myself and others around me. I imagine how good that feels. I am happy to be able to sense how good that feels.

Now let's focus on my ideal outcome which is becoming ageless. I breathe deeply and fully and know that as I do, I am welcoming the happy reality I seek. I am more than a number. I imagine that every breath I take brings more and more goodness into my life. Every breath I release removes what I no longer want in my life, easily and effortlessly. I am becoming lighter and lighter as I release tensions, past disappointments, and old sorrows. These emotions and feelings no longer serve me. Releasing these feelings leaves so much more space for the good that awaits me. My chronological age is just a number.

As I read this Hypnotic Narrative, I am aware that the words I see on this page are creating energy forms that are being created just for me. I feel my eyelids getting heavy as the power of these moments of creation becomes more real to me. I feel a warm, dreamy relaxation moving through my body as my eyes take in these words. I feel it now. And I know that this feeling brings with it the growing likelihood of my ideal outcome finding me. I am the age I choose to be.

As I continue to breathe deeply, I imagine myself moving or floating down a set of stairs. As I float down the stairs, I become more and more relaxed. I realize that I can reach an hypnotic state with my eyes open, even though it's becoming harder and harder to keep my eyes open as I become more and more relaxed. I am ageless.

As I continue to breathe deeply, I feel all cares and worries leave my body. I feel at peace and at ease, at one with the Universe and with my central goal. If I were to close my eyes for a moment, I could feel my energy coalescing with my ideal outcome. As my goal and I become one, the outer reality of that goal comes closer to fruition. I am eternally youthful.

I can feel my body relaxing more and more. I am more than a number. I realize that becoming or attracting whatever I want, is as easy as relaxing, opening myself to that possibility, and allowing that reality into my world. My chronological age is just a number. This new reality can feel a bit odd, new, and good all at the same time. I allow myself to sense the twinkle of happiness I feel about this ideal outcome. I allow myself to anticipate the pleasure that comes to myself and others as I reach my goal. I know that struggle is pointless and so unnecessary once I truly decide what I want, and simply invite the reality of being the age I choose to be into my life.

I truly look forward to improved health and improved relationships, now that I realize that struggle is needless and counter-productive to reaching my goal of becoming ageless. As I continue to allow myself to feel how good this new reality is for me, I commit to using my EOSH sessions daily to give this new reality even more life.

As I continue to breathe deeply, I feel myself expanding energetically, breathing freely, releasing

any remaining old tensions, and moving closer and closer to achieving my ideal outcome. I am who I choose to be.

As I continue to allow myself to become one with my goal, I have a sense of peace that seems to erase any worries or fears I may have had awhile ago. I feel as if I've created a safe space in which to focus on achieving my goal without struggle or strife. I want this feeling of peace and inner quiet to stay with me throughout the day and decide to reinforce this wonderful feeling whenever you can today. I am looking forward to refocusing on my goals again and again throughout the day.

I am grateful to be able to enlist my inner genius to help me to achieve my goal. I am more than a number. I am happy and confident that achieving my goal is right around the corner. I am certain that at my moment of perfect readiness, my goal will be achieved.

As I look around, I remember where I am. I smile to realize how deeply involved I've become in my EOSH Primary Hypnotic Narrative. My body feels

relaxed; I have a sense of otherworldliness, sort of out of space and time. I feel good. I am happy to be alive and happy to be here and happy to be me. I am grateful for this experience and look forward to the next time.

I realize it's time to return to my outer reality. As I take a final deep and cleansing breath, I feel my attention and focus returning to the world around me. It's time to be back to reality and it's good to be back. I will keep watch today for all of the goodness that's headed my way.

CONFIDENCE BUILDER

Breathing deeply, I relax my shoulders, my jaw, and the corners of my mouth. My hands feel pleasantly heavy and I lay them on my knees. I can feel how heavy they seem. I breathe deeply and imagine my life as a canvas on which I will be painting today. I can imagine painting the beautiful picture that my life can be.

I believe that I am empowered to create miracles in my life. As I accept this, that reality awakens and begins to form as part of my belief system. I imagine

155

how good it feels to be a magnet for all good things, all good events and all good people. I allow myself to sense how happy I am becoming, as a person whose energy attracts all goodness to myself and others around me. I imagine how good that feels. I am happy to be able to sense how good that feels.

Now let's focus on my ideal outcome which is building confidence. I breathe deeply and fully and know that as I do, I am welcoming the happy reality I seek. I am strong and brave. I imagine that every breath I take brings more and more goodness into my life. Every breath I release removes what I no longer want in my life, easily and effortlessly. I am becoming lighter and lighter as I release tensions, past disappointments, and old sorrows. These emotions and feelings no longer serve me. Releasing these feelings leaves so much more space for the good that awaits me. I am competent.

As I read this Hypnotic Narrative, I am aware that the words I see on this page are creating energy forms that are being created just for me. I feel my eyelids getting heavy as the power of these moments

of creation becomes more real to me. I feel a warm, dreamy relaxation moving through my body as my eyes take in these words. I feel it now. And I know that this feeling brings with it the growing likelihood of my ideal outcome finding me. I am capable of all tasks required of me.

As I continue to breathe deeply, I imagine myself moving or floating down a set of stairs. As I float down the stairs, I become more and more relaxed. I realize that I can reach an hypnotic state with my eyes open, even though it's becoming harder and harder to keep my eyes open as I become more and more relaxed. I exude confidence.

As I continue to breathe deeply, I feel all cares and worries leave my body. I feel at peace and at ease, at one with the Universe and with my central goal. If I were to close my eyes for a moment, I could feel my energy coalescing with my ideal outcome. As my goal and I become one, the outer reality of that goal comes closer to fruition. I am genuinely confident in my abilities.

I can feel my body relaxing more and more. Everyone remarks how confident I am. I realize that becoming or attracting whatever I want, is as easy as relaxing, opening myself to that possibility, and allowing that reality into my world. I am strong and brave. This new reality can feel a bit odd, new, and good all at the same time. I allow myself to sense the twinkle of happiness I feel about this ideal outcome. I allow myself to anticipate the pleasure that comes to myself and others as I reach my goal. I know that struggle is pointless and so unnecessary once I truly decide what I want, and simply invite the reality of bringing more confidence into my life.

I truly look forward to improved health and improved relationships, now that I realize that struggle is needless and counter-productive to reaching my goal of building more confidence. As I continue to allow myself to feel how good this new reality is for me, I commit to using my EOSH sessions daily to give this new reality even more life.

As I continue to breathe deeply, I feel myself expanding energetically, breathing freely, releasing

any remaining old tensions, and moving closer and closer to achieving my ideal outcome. I am capable of handling all tasks required of me.

As I continue to allow myself to become one with my goal, I have a sense of peace that seems to erase any worries or fears I may have had awhile ago. I feel as if I've created a safe space in which to focus on achieving my goal without struggle or strife. I want this feeling of peace and inner quiet to stay with me throughout the day and decide to reinforce this wonderful feeling whenever you can today. I am looking forward to refocusing on my goals again and again throughout the day.

I am grateful to be able to enlist my inner genius to help me to achieve my goal. I exude confidence. I am happy and confident that achieving my goal is right around the corner. I am certain that at my moment of perfect readiness, my goal will be achieved.

As I look around, I remember where I am. I smile to realize how deeply involved I've become in my EOSH Primary Hypnotic Narrative. My body feels

relaxed; I have a sense of otherworldliness, sort of out of space and time. I feel good. I am happy to be alive and happy to be here and happy to be me. I am grateful for this experience and look forward to the next time.

I realize it's time to return to my outer reality. As I take a final deep and cleansing breath, I feel my attention and focus returning to the world around me. It's time to be back to reality and it's good to be back. I will keep watch today for all of the goodness that's headed my way.

CONTROL ALCOHOL

Breathing deeply, I relax my shoulders, my jaw, and the corners of my mouth. My hands feel pleasantly heavy and I lay them on my knees. I can feel how heavy they seem. I breathe deeply and imagine my life as a canvas on which I will be painting today. I can imagine painting the beautiful picture that my life can be.

I believe that I am empowered to create miracles in my life. As I accept this, that reality awakens and begins to form as part of my belief system. I imagine how good it feels to be a magnet for all good things, all good events and all good people. I allow myself to sense how happy I am becoming, as a person whose energy attracts all goodness to myself and others around me. I imagine how good that feels. I am happy to be able to sense how good that feels.

Now let's focus on my ideal outcome which is controlling alcohol. I breathe deeply and fully and know that as I do, I am welcoming the happy reality I seek. Alcohol has no hold on me. I imagine that every breath I take brings more and more goodness into my life. Every breath I release removes what I no longer want in my life, easily and effortlessly. I am becoming lighter and lighter as I release tensions, past disappointments, and old sorrows. These emotions and feelings no longer serve me. Releasing these feelings leaves so much more space for the good that awaits me. I am free of any desire for alcohol.

As I read this Hypnotic Narrative, I am aware that the words I see on this page are creating energy forms that are being created just for me. I feel my eyelids getting heavy as the power of these moments of creation becomes more real to me. I feel a warm, dreamy relaxation moving through my body as my eyes take in these words. I feel it now. And I know that this feeling brings with it the growing likelihood of my ideal outcome finding me. Alcohol consumption is hard on my body and I choose to be kind to my body.

As I continue to breathe deeply, I imagine myself moving or floating down a set of stairs. As I float down the stairs, I become more and more relaxed. I realize that I can reach an hypnotic state with my eyes open, even though it's becoming harder and harder to keep my eyes open as I become more and more relaxed. I love the way that my sober brain works.

As I continue to breathe deeply, I feel all cares and worries leave my body. I feel at peace and at ease, at one with the Universe and with my central goal. If I were to close my eyes for a moment, I could feel my energy coalescing with my ideal outcome. As my goal and I become one, the outer reality of that goal comes closer to fruition. I always do what's best for my body.

I can feel my body relaxing more and more. I love the way that my sober body feels. I realize that becoming or attracting whatever I want, is as easy as relaxing, opening myself to that possibility, and allowing that reality into my world. I love feeling strong and free. This new reality can feel a bit odd, new, and good all at the same time. I allow myself to sense the twinkle of happiness I feel about this ideal outcome. I allow myself to anticipate the pleasure that comes to myself and others as I reach my goal. I know that struggle is pointless and so unnecessary once I truly decide what I want, and simply invite the reality of controlling alcohol into my life.

I truly look forward to improved health and improved relationships, now that I realize that struggle is needless and counter-productive to reaching my goal of controlling alcohol. As I continue to allow myself to feel how good this new reality is for me, I commit to using my EOSH sessions daily to give this new reality even more life.

As I continue to breathe deeply, I feel myself expanding energetically, breathing freely, releasing any remaining old tensions, and moving closer and closer to achieving my ideal outcome. I am free of any desire for alcohol.

As I continue to allow myself to become one with my goal, I have a sense of peace that seems to erase any worries or fears I may have had awhile ago. I feel as if I've created a safe space in which to focus on achieving my goal without struggle or strife. I want this feeling of peace and inner quiet to stay with me throughout the day and decide to reinforce this wonderful feeling whenever you can today. I am looking forward to refocusing on my goals again and again throughout the day.

I am grateful to be able to enlist my inner genius to help me to achieve my goal. I love the way my healthy body feels. I am happy and confident that achieving my goal is right around the corner. I am certain that at my moment of perfect readiness, my goal will be achieved.

As I look around, I remember where I am. I smile to realize how deeply involved I've become in my EOSH Primary Hypnotic Narrative. My body feels relaxed; I have a sense of otherworldliness, sort of out of space and time. I feel good. I am happy to be alive and happy to be here and happy to be me. I am grateful for this experience and look forward to the next time.

I realize it's time to return to my outer reality. As I take a final deep and cleansing breath, I feel my attention and focus returning to the world around me. It's time to be back to reality and it's good to be back. I will keep watch today for all of the goodness that's headed my way.

EASY RELAXATION

Breathing deeply, I relax my shoulders, my jaw, and the corners of my mouth. My hands feel pleasantly heavy and I lay them on my knees. I can feel how heavy they seem. I breathe deeply and imagine my life as a canvas on which I will be painting today. I can imagine painting the beautiful picture that my life can be.

I believe that I am empowered to create miracles in my life. As I accept this, that reality awakens and begins to form as part of my belief system. I imagine how good it feels to be a magnet for all good things, all good events and all good people. I allow myself to sense how happy I am becoming, as a person whose energy attracts all goodness to myself and others around me. I imagine how good that feels. I am happy to be able to sense how good that feels.

Now let's focus on my ideal outcome which is easy relaxation. I breathe deeply and fully and know that as I do, I am welcoming the happy reality I seek. I am so lucky to be able to relax so easily. I imagine that every breath I take brings more and more goodness into my life. Every breath I release removes what I no longer want in my life, easily and effortlessly. I am becoming lighter and lighter as I release tensions, past disappointments, and old sorrows. These emotions and feelings no longer serve me. Releasing these feelings leaves so much more space for the good that awaits me. I can leave behind a hectic day easily.

As I read this Hypnotic Narrative, I am aware that the words I see on this page are creating energy forms that are being created just for me. I feel my eyelids getting heavy as the power of these moments of creation becomes more real to me. I feel a warm, dreamy relaxation moving through my body as my eyes take in these words. I feel it now. And I know that this feeling brings with it the growing likelihood of my ideal outcome finding me. My work day ends as soon as I leave work.

As I continue to breathe deeply, I imagine myself moving or floating down a set of stairs. As I float down the stairs, I become more and more relaxed. I realize that I can reach an hypnotic state with my eyes open, even though it's becoming harder and harder to keep my eyes open as I become more and more relaxed. I am patient with my children at all times.

167

As I continue to breathe deeply, I feel all cares and worries leave my body. I feel at peace and at ease, at one with the Universe and with my central goal. If I were to close my eyes for a moment, I could feel my energy coalescing with my ideal outcome. As my goal and I become one, the outer reality of that goal comes closer to fruition. My mind turns off when I tell it to.

I can feel my body relaxing more and more. I am able to play as hard as I work. I realize that becoming or attracting whatever I want, is as easy as relaxing, opening myself to that possibility, and allowing that reality into my world. I am so lucky to be able to relax so easily. This new reality can feel a bit odd, new, and good all at the same time. I allow myself to sense the twinkle of happiness I feel about this ideal outcome. I allow myself to anticipate the pleasure that comes to myself and others as I reach my goal. I know that struggle is pointless and so unnecessary once I truly decide what I want, and simply invite the reality of easy relaxation into my life.

I truly look forward to improved health and improved relationships, now that I realize that struggle is needless and counter-productive to reaching my goal of achieving easy relaxation. As I continue to allow myself to feel how good this new reality is for me, I commit to using my EOSH sessions daily to give this new reality even more life.

As I continue to breathe deeply, I feel myself expanding energetically, breathing freely, releasing any remaining old tensions, and moving closer and closer to achieving my ideal outcome. I can leave a hectic day behind easily.

As I continue to allow myself to become one with my goal, I have a sense of peace that seems to erase any worries or fears I may have had awhile ago. I feel as if I've created a safe space in which to focus on achieving my goal without struggle or strife. I want this feeling of peace and inner quiet to stay with me throughout the day and decide to reinforce this wonderful feeling whenever you can today. I am looking forward to refocusing on my goals again and again throughout the day.

I am grateful to be able to enlist my inner genius to help me to achieve my goal. My work day ends as soon as I get home. I am happy and confident that achieving my goal is right around the corner. I am certain that at my moment of perfect readiness, my goal will be achieved.

As I look around, I remember where I am. I smile to realize how deeply involved I've become in my EOSH Primary Hypnotic Narrative. My body feels relaxed; I have a sense of otherworldliness, sort of out of space and time. I feel good. I am happy to be alive and happy to be here and happy to be me. I am grateful for this experience and look forward to the next time.

I realize it's time to return to my outer reality. As I take a final deep and cleansing breath, I feel my attention and focus returning to the world around me. It's time to be back to reality and it's good to be back. I will keep watch today for all of the goodness that's headed my way.

EXERCISE IS FUN

Breathing deeply, I relax my shoulders, my jaw, and the corners of my mouth. My hands feel pleasantly heavy and I lay them on my knees. I can feel how heavy they seem. I breathe deeply and imagine my life as a canvas on which I will be painting today. I can imagine painting the beautiful picture that my life can be.

I believe that I am empowered to create miracles in my life. As I accept this, that reality awakens and begins to form as part of my belief system. I imagine how good it feels to be a magnet for all good things, all good events and all good people. I allow myself to sense how happy I am becoming, as a person whose energy attracts all goodness to myself and others around me. I imagine how good that feels. I am happy to be able to sense how good that feels.

Now let's focus on my ideal outcome which is enjoying exercise. I breathe deeply and fully and know that as I do, I am welcoming the happy reality I seek. Exercise is fun for me. I imagine that every breath I take brings more and more goodness into my life. Every breath I release removes what I no longer want in my life, easily and effortlessly. I am becoming lighter and lighter as I release tensions, past disappointments, and old sorrows. These emotions and feelings no longer serve me. Releasing these feelings leaves so much more space for the good that awaits me. Exercise feels good.

As I read this Hypnotic Narrative, I am aware that the words I see on this page are creating energy forms that are being created just for me. I feel my eyelids getting heavy as the power of these moments of creation becomes more real to me. I feel a warm, dreamy relaxation moving through my body as my eyes take in these words. I feel it now. And I know that this feeling brings with it the growing likelihood of my ideal outcome finding me. I love the way my body feels when I exercise.

As I continue to breathe deeply, I imagine myself moving or floating down a set of stairs. As I float down the stairs, I become more and more relaxed. I realize that I can reach an hypnotic state with my

eyes open, even though it's becoming harder and harder to keep my eyes open as I become more and more relaxed. I know that exercise is good for my body.

As I continue to breathe deeply, I feel all cares and worries leave my body. I feel at peace and at ease, at one with the Universe and with my central goal. If I were to close my eyes for a moment, I could feel my energy coalescing with my ideal outcome. As my goal and I become one, the outer reality of that goal comes closer to fruition. I have fun no matter what kind of exercise I am doing.

I can feel my body relaxing more and more. I look forward to exercising. I realize that becoming or attracting whatever I want, is as easy as relaxing, opening myself to that possibility, and allowing that reality into my world. Exercise is fun. This new reality can feel a bit odd, new, and good all at the same time. I allow myself to sense the twinkle of happiness I feel about this ideal outcome. I allow myself to anticipate the pleasure that comes to myself and others as I reach my goal. I know that struggle is pointless and so unnecessary once I truly decide what I want, and simply invite the reality of [Affirmation Here] into my life.

I truly look forward to improved health and improved relationships, now that I realize that struggle is needless and counter-productive to reaching my goal of enjoying exercise. As I continue to allow myself to feel how good this new reality is for me, I commit to using my EOSH sessions daily to give this new reality even more life.

As I continue to breathe deeply, I feel myself expanding energetically, breathing freely, releasing any remaining old tensions, and moving closer and closer to achieving my ideal outcome. Exercise feels good.

As I continue to allow myself to become one with my goal, I have a sense of peace that seems to erase any worries or fears I may have had awhile ago. I feel as if I've created a safe space in which to focus on achieving my goal without struggle or strife. I want this feeling of peace and inner quiet to stay with me throughout the day and decide to reinforce this wonderful feeling whenever you can today. I am looking forward to refocusing on my goals again and again throughout the day.

I am grateful to be able to enlist my inner genius to help me to achieve my goal. I love the way my body feels when I exercise. I am happy and confident that achieving my goal is right around the corner. I am certain that at my moment of perfect readiness, my goal will be achieved.

As I look around, I remember where I am. I smile to realize how deeply involved I've become in my EOSH Primary Hypnotic Narrative. My body feels relaxed; I have a sense of otherworldliness, sort of out of space and time. I feel good. I am happy to be alive and happy to be here and happy to be me. I am grateful for this experience and look forward to the next time.

I realize it's time to return to my outer reality. As I take a final deep and cleansing breath, I feel my attention and focus returning to the world around me. It's time to be back to reality and it's good to be

back. I will keep watch today for all of the goodness that's headed my way.

I AM ADVENTUROUS

Breathing deeply, I relax my shoulders, my jaw, and the corners of my mouth. My hands feel pleasantly heavy and I lay them on my knees. I can feel how heavy they seem. I breathe deeply and imagine my life as a canvas on which I will be painting today. I can imagine painting the beautiful picture that my life can be.

I believe that I am empowered to create miracles in my life. As I accept this, that reality awakens and begins to form as part of my belief system. I imagine how good it feels to be a magnet for all good things, all good events and all good people. I allow myself to sense how happy I am becoming, as a person whose energy attracts all goodness to myself and others around me. I imagine how good that feels. I am happy to be able to sense how good that feels.

Now let's focus on my ideal outcome which is to become more adventurous. I breathe deeply and fully and know that as I do, I am welcoming the happy reality I seek. I am always up for a new adventure. I imagine that every breath I take brings more and more goodness into my life. Every breath I release removes what I no longer want in my life, easily and effortlessly. I am becoming lighter and lighter as I release tensions, past disappointments, and old sorrows. These emotions and feelings no longer serve me. Releasing these feelings leaves so much more space for the good that awaits me. I am the first one to sign up for something new.

As I read this Hypnotic Narrative, I am aware that the words I see on this page are creating energy forms that are being created just for me. I feel my eyelids getting heavy as the power of these moments of creation becomes more real to me. I feel a warm, dreamy relaxation moving through my body as my eyes take in these words. I feel it now. And I know that this feeling brings with it the growing likelihood of my ideal outcome finding me. I feel safe in new situations.

As I continue to breathe deeply, I imagine myself moving or floating down a set of stairs. As I float down the stairs, I become more and more relaxed. I realize that I can reach an hypnotic state with my eyes open, even though it's becoming harder and harder to keep my eyes open as I become more and more relaxed. I love new games, adventure vacations, and meeting new people.

As I continue to breathe deeply, I feel all cares and worries leave my body. I feel at peace and at ease, at one with the Universe and with my central goal. If I were to close my eyes for a moment, I could feel my energy coalescing with my ideal outcome. As my goal and I become one, the outer reality of that goal comes closer to fruition. There's nothing wrong with the norm but the new is more interesting to me.

I can feel my body relaxing more and more. I like feeling sure in new situations. I realize that becoming or attracting whatever I want, is as easy as relaxing, opening myself to that possibility, and allowing that reality into my world. I feel safe in new situations. This new reality can feel a bit odd, new, and good all at the same time. I allow myself to sense the twinkle of happiness I feel about this ideal outcome. I allow myself to anticipate the pleasure that comes to myself and others as I reach my goal. I know that struggle is pointless and so unnecessary once I truly decide what I want, and simply invite the reality of being more adventurous into my life.

I truly look forward to improved health and improved relationships, now that I realize that struggle is needless and counter-productive to reaching my goal of being more adventurous. As I continue to allow myself to feel how good this new reality is for me, I commit to using my EOSH sessions daily to give this new reality even more life.

As I continue to breathe deeply, I feel myself expanding energetically, breathing freely, releasing any remaining old tensions, and moving closer and closer to achieving my ideal outcome. I like getting lost so I can be found.

As I continue to allow myself to become one with my goal, I have a sense of peace that seems to erase any worries or fears I may have had awhile ago. I

179

feel as if I've created a safe space in which to focus on achieving my goal without struggle or strife. I want this feeling of peace and inner quiet to stay with me throughout the day and decide to reinforce this wonderful feeling whenever you can today. I am looking forward to refocusing on my goals again and again throughout the day.

I am grateful to be able to enlist my inner genius to help me to achieve my goal. I am always up for a new adventure. I am happy and confident that achieving my goal is right around the corner. I am certain that at my moment of perfect readiness, my goal will be achieved.

As I look around, I remember where I am. I smile to realize how deeply involved I've become in my EOSH Primary Hypnotic Narrative. My body feels relaxed; I have a sense of otherworldliness, sort of out of space and time. I feel good. I am happy to be alive and happy to be here and happy to be me. I am grateful for this experience and look forward to the next time.

I realize it's time to return to my outer reality. As I take a final deep and cleansing breath, I feel my attention and focus returning to the world around me. It's time to be back to reality and it's good to be back. I will keep watch today for all of the goodness that's headed my way.

IMPROVED DIGESTION

Breathing deeply, I relax my shoulders, my jaw, and the corners of my mouth. My hands feel pleasantly heavy and I lay them on my knees. I can feel how heavy they seem. I breathe deeply and imagine my life as a canvas on which I will be painting today. I can imagine painting the beautiful picture that my life can be.

I believe that I am empowered to create miracles in my life. As I accept this, that reality awakens and begins to form as part of my belief system. I imagine how good it feels to be a magnet for all good things, all good events and all good people. I allow myself to sense how happy I am becoming, as a person whose energy attracts all goodness to myself and

181

others around me. I imagine how good that feels. I am happy to be able to sense how good that feels.

Now let's focus on my ideal outcome which is improved digestion. I breathe deeply and fully and know that as I do, I am welcoming the happy reality I seek. I imagine that every breath I take brings more and more goodness into my life. Every breath I release removes what I no longer want in my life, easily and effortlessly. I am becoming lighter and lighter as I release tensions, past disappointments, and old sorrows. These emotions and feelings no longer serve me. Releasing these feelings leaves so much more space for the good that awaits me. My body digests food easily.

As I read this Hypnotic Narrative, I am aware that the words I see on this page are creating energy forms that are being created just for me. I feel my eyelids getting heavy as the power of these moments of creation becomes more real to me. I feel a warm, dreamy relaxation moving through my body as my eyes take in these words. I feel it now. And I know that this feeling brings with it the growing likelihood

of my ideal outcome finding me. I eat, assimilate, and eliminate food optimally.

As I continue to breathe deeply, I imagine myself moving or floating down a set of stairs. As I float down the stairs, I become more and more relaxed. I realize that I can reach an hypnotic state with my eyes open, even though it's becoming harder and harder to keep my eyes open as I become more and more relaxed. I choose to eat healthy food.

As I continue to breathe deeply, I feel all cares and worries leave my body. I feel at peace and at ease, at one with the Universe and with my central goal. If I were to close my eyes for a moment, I could feel my energy coalescing with my ideal outcome. As my goal and I become one, the outer reality of that goal comes closer to fruition. I have the digestive system of a young child.

I can feel my body relaxing more and more. I can eat like a horse and digest like one too. I realize that becoming or attracting whatever I want, is as easy as relaxing, opening myself to that possibility, and allowing that reality into my world. My metabolism is excellent. This new reality can feel a bit odd, new, and good all at the same time. I allow myself to sense the twinkle of happiness I feel about this ideal outcome. I allow myself to anticipate the pleasure that comes to myself and others as I reach my goal. I know that struggle is pointless and so unnecessary once I truly decide what I want, and simply invite the reality of improved digestion into my life.

I truly look forward to improved health and improved relationships, now that I realize that struggle is needless and counter-productive to reaching my goal of improved digestion. As I continue to allow myself to feel how good this new reality is for me, I commit to using my EOSH sessions daily to give this new reality even more life.

As I continue to breathe deeply, I feel myself expanding energetically, breathing freely, releasing any remaining old tensions, and moving closer and closer to achieving my ideal outcome. My entire digestive tract works perfectly.

As I continue to allow myself to become one with my goal, I have a sense of peace that seems to erase

any worries or fears I may have had awhile ago. I feel as if I've created a safe space in which to focus on achieving my goal without struggle or strife. I want this feeling of peace and inner quiet to stay with me throughout the day and decide to reinforce this wonderful feeling whenever you can today. I am looking forward to refocusing on my goals again and again throughout the day.

I am grateful to be able to enlist my inner genius to help me to achieve my goal. My body digests food easily. I am happy and confident that achieving my goal is right around the corner. I am certain that at my moment of perfect readiness, my goal will be achieved.

As I look around, I remember where I am. I smile to realize how deeply involved I've become in my EOSH Primary Hypnotic Narrative. My body feels relaxed; I have a sense of otherworldliness, sort of out of space and time. I feel good. I am happy to be alive and happy to be here and happy to be me. I am grateful for this experience and look forward to the next time.

I realize it's time to return to my outer reality. As I take a final deep and cleansing breath, I feel my attention and focus returning to the world around me. It's time to be back to reality and it's good to be back. I will keep watch today for all of the goodness that's headed my way.

IMPROVED EYESIGHT

Breathing deeply, I relax my shoulders, my jaw, and the corners of my mouth. My hands feel pleasantly heavy and I lay them on my knees. I can feel how heavy they seem. I breathe deeply and imagine my life as a canvas on which I will be painting today. I can imagine painting the beautiful picture that my life can be.

I believe that I am empowered to create miracles in my life. As I accept this, that reality awakens and begins to form as part of my belief system. I imagine how good it feels to be a magnet for all good things, all good events and all good people. I allow myself to sense how happy I am becoming, as a person whose energy attracts all goodness to myself and

others around me. I imagine how good that feels. I am happy to be able to sense how good that feels.

Now let's focus on my ideal outcome which is improved eyesight. I breathe deeply and fully and know that as I do, I am welcoming the happy reality I seek. I see clearly. I imagine that every breath I take brings more and more goodness into my life. Every breath I release removes what I no longer want in my life, easily and effortlessly. I am becoming lighter and lighter as I release tensions, past disappointments, and old sorrows. These emotions and feelings no longer serve me. Releasing these feelings leaves so much more space for the good that awaits me. I have the eyesight of an eagle.

As I read this Hypnotic Narrative, I am aware that the words I see on this page are creating energy forms that are being created just for me. I feel my eyelids getting heavy as the power of these moments of creation becomes more real to me. I feel a warm, dreamy relaxation moving through my body as my eyes take in these words. I feel it now. And I know that this feeling brings with it the growing likelihood

of my ideal outcome finding me. I am lucky to be able to see so well.

As I continue to breathe deeply, I imagine myself moving or floating down a set of stairs. As I float down the stairs, I become more and more relaxed. I realize that I can reach an hypnotic state with my eyes open, even though it's becoming harder and harder to keep my eyes open as I become more and more relaxed. I am careful of my eyes and choose not to overwork them.

As I continue to breathe deeply, I feel all cares and worries leave my body. I feel at peace and at ease, at one with the Universe and with my central goal. If I were to close my eyes for a moment, I could feel my energy coalescing with my ideal outcome. As my goal and I become one, the outer reality of that goal comes closer to fruition. My eyes are my most valued possessions.

I can feel my body relaxing more and more. I love to see in the distance as well as up close. I realize that becoming or attracting whatever I want, is as easy as relaxing, opening myself to that possibility, and allowing that reality into my world. Reading and watching television are major pleasures for me. This new reality can feel a bit odd, new, and good all at the same time   I allow myself to sense the twinkle of happiness I feel about this ideal outcome. I allow myself to anticipate the pleasure that comes to myself and others as I reach my goal. I know that struggle is pointless and so unnecessary once I truly decide what I want, and simply invite the reality of improved eyesight into my life.

I truly look forward to improved health and improved relationships, now that I realize that struggle is needless and counter-productive to reaching my goal of improved eyesight. As I continue to allow myself to feel how good this new reality is for me, I commit to using my EOSH sessions daily to give this new reality even more life.

As I continue to breathe deeply, I feel myself expanding energetically, breathing freely, releasing any remaining old tensions, and moving closer and closer to achieving my ideal outcome. I love my eyes.

189

As I continue to allow myself to become one with my goal, I have a sense of peace that seems to erase any worries or fears I may have had awhile ago. I feel as if I've created a safe space in which to focus on achieving my goal without struggle or strife. I want this feeling of peace and inner quiet to stay with me throughout the day and decide to reinforce this wonderful feeling whenever you can today. I am looking forward to refocusing on my goals again and again throughout the day.

I am grateful to be able to enlist my inner genius to help me to achieve my goal. I am lucky to see so well. I am happy and confident that achieving my goal is right around the corner. I am certain that at my moment of perfect readiness, my goal will be achieved.

As I look around, I remember where I am. I smile to realize how deeply involved I've become in my EOSH Primary Hypnotic Narrative. My body feels relaxed; I have a sense of otherworldliness, sort of out of space and time. I feel good. I am happy to be alive and happy to be here and happy to be me. I am grateful for this experience and look forward to the next time.

I realize it's time to return to my outer reality. As I take a final deep and cleansing breath, I feel my attention and focus returning to the world around me. It's time to be back to reality and it's good to be back. I will keep watch today for all of the goodness that's headed my way.

LOSE WEIGHT NOW

Breathing deeply, I relax my shoulders, my jaw, and the corners of my mouth. My hands feel pleasantly heavy and I lay them on my knees. I can feel how heavy they seem. I breathe deeply and imagine my life as a canvas on which I will be painting today. I can imagine painting the beautiful picture that my life can be.

I believe that I am empowered to create miracles in my life. As I accept this, that reality awakens and begins to form as part of my belief system. I imagine how good it feels to be a magnet for all good things,

191

all good events and all good people. I allow myself to sense how happy I am becoming, as a person whose energy attracts all goodness to myself and others around me. I imagine how good that feels. I am happy to be able to sense how good that feels.

Now let's focus on my ideal outcome. I breathe deeply and fully and know that as I do, I am welcoming the happy reality I seek. I enjoy foods that taste good and that are good for me. I imagine that every breath I take brings more and more goodness into my life. Every breath I release removes what I no longer want in my life, easily and effortlessly. I am becoming lighter and lighter as I release tensions, past disappointments, and old sorrows. These emotions and feelings no longer serve me. Releasing these feelings leaves so much more space for the good that awaits me. I enjoy salads, chicken, and fish.

As I read this Hypnotic Narrative, I am aware that the words I see on this page are creating energy forms that are being created just for me. I feel my eyelids getting heavy as the power of these moments

of creation becomes more real to me. I feel a warm, dreamy relaxation moving through my body as my eyes take in these words. I feel it now. And I know that this feeling brings with it the growing likelihood of my ideal outcome finding me. My digestive system works perfectly.

As I continue to breathe deeply, I imagine myself moving or floating down a set of stairs. As I float down the stairs, I become more and more relaxed. I realize that I can reach an hypnotic state with my eyes open, even though it's becoming harder and harder to keep my eyes open as I become more and more relaxed. I digest, assimilate and eliminate like a healthy child.

As I continue to breathe deeply, I feel all cares and worries leave my body. I feel at peace and at ease, at one with the Universe and with my central goal. If I were to close my eyes for a moment, I could feel my energy coalescing with my ideal outcome. As my goal and I become one, the outer reality of that goal comes closer to fruition. My body releases excess weight and water easily.

I can feel my body relaxing more and more. My body is healthy and functions optimally. I realize that becoming or attracting whatever I want, is as easy as relaxing, opening myself to that possibility, and allowing that reality into my world. I can eat what I want and still lose weight easily. This new reality can feel a bit odd, new, and good all at the same time I allow myself to sense the twinkle of happiness I feel about this ideal outcome. I allow myself to anticipate the pleasure that comes to myself and others as I reach my goal. I know that struggle is pointless and so unnecessary once I truly decide what I want, and simply invite the reality of losing weight easily into my life.

I truly look forward to improved health and improved relationships, now that I realize that struggle is needless and counter-productive to reaching my goal of easy weight loss. As I continue to allow myself to feel how good this new reality is for me, I commit to using my EOSH sessions daily to give this new reality even more life.

194

As I continue to breathe deeply, I feel myself expanding energetically, breathing freely, releasing any remaining old tensions, and moving closer and closer to achieving my ideal outcome. I enjoy foods that taste good and that are good for me.

As I continue to allow myself to become one with my goal, I have a sense of peace that seems to erase any worries or fears I may have had awhile ago. I feel as if I've created a safe space in which to focus on achieving my goal without struggle or strife. I want this feeling of peace and inner quiet to stay with me throughout the day and decide to reinforce this wonderful feeling whenever you can today. I am looking forward to refocusing on my goals again and again throughout the day.

I am grateful to be able to enlist my inner genius to help me to achieve my goal. I enjoy salads, chicken and fish. I am happy and confident that achieving my goal is right around the corner. I am certain that at my moment of perfect readiness, my goal will be achieved.

As I look around, I remember where I am. I smile to realize how deeply involved I've become in my EOSH Primary Hypnotic Narrative. My body feels relaxed; I have a sense of otherworldliness, sort of out of space and time. I feel good. I am happy to be alive and happy to be here and happy to be me. I am grateful for this experience and look forward to the next time.

I realize it's time to return to my outer reality. As I take a final deep and cleansing breath, I feel my attention and focus returning to the world around me. It's time to be back to reality and it's good to be back. I will keep watch today for all of the goodness that's headed my way.

MAKINGS FRIENDS EASILY

Breathing deeply, I relax my shoulders, my jaw, and the corners of my mouth. My hands feel pleasantly heavy and I lay them on my knees. I can feel how heavy they seem. I breathe deeply and imagine my life as a canvas on which I will be painting today. I

196

can imagine painting the beautiful picture that my life can be.

I believe that I am empowered to create miracles in my life. As I accept this, that reality awakens and begins to form as part of my belief system. I imagine how good it feels to be a magnet for all good things, all good events and all good people. I allow myself to sense how happy I am becoming, as a person whose energy attracts all goodness to myself and others around me. I imagine how good that feels. I am happy to be able to sense how good that feels.

Now let's focus on my ideal outcome which is making friends easily. I breathe deeply and fully and know that as I do, I am welcoming the happy reality I seek. I enjoy meeting new people and learning about their lives. I imagine that every breath I take brings more and more goodness into my life. Every breath I release removes what I no longer want in my life, easily and effortlessly. I am becoming lighter and lighter as I release tensions, past disappointments, and old sorrows. These emotions and feelings no longer serve me. Releasing these feelings leaves so

197

much more space for the good that awaits me. I really like people.

As I read this Hypnotic Narrative, I am aware that the words I see on this page are creating energy forms that are being created just for me. I feel my eyelids getting heavy as the power of these moments of creation becomes more real to me. I feel a warm, dreamy relaxation moving through my body as my eyes take in these words. I feel it now. And I know that this feeling brings with it the growing likelihood of my ideal outcome finding me. People are fascinating.

As I continue to breathe deeply, I imagine myself moving or floating down a set of stairs. As I float down the stairs, I become more and more relaxed. I realize that I can reach an hypnotic state with my eyes open, even though it's becoming harder and harder to keep my eyes open as I become more and more relaxed. I learn something new from everyone I meet.

As I continue to breathe deeply, I feel all cares and worries leave my body. I feel at peace and at ease, at one with the Universe and with my central goal. If I were to close my eyes for a moment, I could feel my energy coalescing with my ideal outcome. As my goal and I become one, the outer reality of that goal comes closer to fruition. I have time to share with many friends.

I can feel my body relaxing more and more. I love making new friends. I realize that becoming or attracting whatever I want, is as easy as relaxing, opening myself to that possibility, and allowing that reality into my world. Every person I meet is a potential new friend. This new reality can feel a bit odd, new, and good all at the same time. I allow myself to sense the twinkle of happiness I feel about this ideal outcome. I allow myself to anticipate the pleasure that comes to myself and others as I reach my goal. I know that struggle is pointless and so unnecessary once I truly decide what I want, and simply invite the reality of making friends easily into my life.

I truly look forward to improved health and improved relationships, now that I realize that

199

struggle is needless and counter-productive to reaching my goal of making friends easily. As I continue to allow myself to feel how good this new reality is for me, I commit to using my EOSH sessions daily to give this new reality even more life.

As I continue to breathe deeply, I feel myself expanding energetically, breathing freely, releasing any remaining old tensions, and moving closer and closer to achieving my ideal outcome. I really like people.

As I continue to allow myself to become one with my goal, I have a sense of peace that seems to erase any worries or fears I may have had awhile ago. I feel as if I've created a safe space in which to focus on achieving my goal without struggle or strife. I want this feeling of peace and inner quiet to stay with me throughout the day and decide to reinforce this wonderful feeling whenever you can today. I am looking forward to refocusing on my goals again and again throughout the day.

I am grateful to be able to enlist my inner genius to help me to achieve my goal. People are fascinating. I am happy and confident that achieving my goal is right around the corner. I am certain that at my moment of perfect readiness, my goal will be achieved.

As I look around, I remember where I am. I smile to realize how deeply involved I've become in my EOSH Primary Hypnotic Narrative. My body feels relaxed; I have a sense of otherworldliness, sort of out of space and time. I feel good. I am happy to be alive and happy to be here and happy to be me. I am grateful for this experience and look forward to the next time.

I realize it's time to return to my outer reality. As I take a final deep and cleansing breath, I feel my attention and focus returning to the world around me. It's time to be back to reality and it's good to be back. I will keep watch today for all of the goodness that's headed my way.

MEMORY BOOSTER

Breathing deeply, I relax my shoulders, my jaw, and the corners of my mouth. My hands feel pleasantly heavy and I lay them on my knees. I can feel how heavy they seem. I breathe deeply and imagine my life as a canvas on which I will be painting today. I can imagine painting the beautiful picture that my life can be.

I believe that I am empowered to create miracles in my life. As I accept this, that reality awakens and begins to form as part of my belief system. I imagine how good it feels to be a magnet for all good things, all good events and all good people. I allow myself to sense how happy I am becoming, as a person whose energy attracts all goodness to myself and others around me. I imagine how good that feels. I am happy to be able to sense how good that feels.

Now let's focus on my ideal outcome which is an improved memory. I breathe deeply and fully and know that as I do, I am welcoming the happy reality I seek. I have an excellent memory. I imagine that every breath I take brings more and more goodness into my life. Every breath I release removes what I no longer want in my life, easily and effortlessly. I am becoming lighter and lighter as I release tensions, past disappointments, and old sorrows. These emotions and feelings no longer serve me. Releasing these feelings leaves so much more space for the good that awaits me. I can remember phone numbers from my childhood.

As I read this Hypnotic Narrative, I am aware that the words I see on this page are creating energy forms that are being created just for me. I feel my eyelids getting heavy as the power of these moments of creation becomes more real to me. I feel a warm, dreamy relaxation moving through my body as my eyes take in these words. I feel it now. And I know that this feeling brings with it the growing likelihood of my ideal outcome finding me. I love trivia and jokes and remember lots of them.

As I continue to breathe deeply, I imagine myself moving or floating down a set of stairs. As I float down the stairs, I become more and more relaxed. I realize that I can reach an hypnotic state with my eyes open, even though it's becoming harder and harder to keep my eyes open as I become more and more relaxed. I have the memory of an elephant.

As I continue to breathe deeply, I feel all cares and worries leave my body. I feel at peace and at ease, at one with the Universe and with my central goal. If I were to close my eyes for a moment, I could feel my energy coalescing with my ideal outcome. As my goal and I become one, the outer reality of that goal comes closer to fruition. I can place names and faces easily.

I can feel my body relaxing more and more. My mind is facile and remembers everything easily. I realize that becoming or attracting whatever I want, is as easy as relaxing, opening myself to that possibility, and allowing that reality into my world. I have an excellent memory. This new reality can feel a bit odd, new, and good all at the same time. I allow myself to sense the twinkle of happiness I feel about this ideal outcome. I allow myself to anticipate the pleasure that comes to myself and others as I reach my goal. I know that struggle is pointless and so unnecessary once I truly decide what I want, and simply invite the reality of improved memory into my life.

I truly look forward to improved health and improved relationships, now that I realize that struggle is needless and counter-productive to reaching my goal of improved memory. As I continue to allow myself to feel how good this new reality is for me, I commit to using my EOSH sessions daily to give this new reality even more life.

As I continue to breathe deeply, I feel myself expanding energetically, breathing freely, releasing any remaining old tensions, and moving closer and closer to achieving my ideal outcome. I can remember phone numbers from my childhood.

As I continue to allow myself to become one with my goal, I have a sense of peace that seems to erase any worries or fears I may have had awhile ago. I feel as if I've created a safe space in which to focus on achieving my goal without struggle or strife. I want this feeling of peace and inner quiet to stay with me throughout the day and decide to reinforce this wonderful feeling whenever you can today. I am looking forward to refocusing on my goals again and again throughout the day.

I am grateful to be able to enlist my inner genius to help me to achieve my goal. I have the memory of an elephant. I am happy and confident that achieving my goal is right around the corner. I am certain that at my moment of perfect readiness, my goal will be achieved.

As I look around, I remember where I am. I smile to realize how deeply involved I've become in my EOSH Primary Hypnotic Narrative. My body feels relaxed; I have a sense of otherworldliness, sort of out of space and time. I feel good. I am happy to be alive and happy to be here and happy to be me. I am grateful for this experience and look forward to the next time.

I realize it's time to return to my outer reality. As I take a final deep and cleansing breath, I feel my attention and focus returning to the world around me. It's time to be back to reality and it's good to be

back. I will keep watch today for all of the goodness that's headed my way.

PROCRASTINATION BE GONE

Breathing deeply, I relax my shoulders, my jaw, and the corners of my mouth. My hands feel pleasantly heavy and I lay them on my knees. I can feel how heavy they seem. I breathe deeply and imagine my life as a canvas on which I will be painting today. I can imagine painting the beautiful picture that my life can be.

I believe that I am empowered to create miracles in my life. As I accept this, that reality awakens and begins to form as part of my belief system. I imagine how good it feels to be a magnet for all good things, all good events and all good people. I allow myself to sense how happy I am becoming, as a person whose energy attracts all goodness to myself and others around me. I imagine how good that feels. I am happy to be able to sense how good that feels.

Now let's focus on my ideal outcome which is getting free of procrastination. I breathe deeply and fully and know that as I do, I am welcoming the happy reality I seek. I take care of things as soon as they come up. I imagine that every breath I take brings more and more goodness into my life. Every breath I release removes what I no longer want in my life, easily and effortlessly. I am becoming lighter and lighter as I release tensions, past disappointments, and old sorrows. These emotions and feelings no longer serve me. Releasing these feelings leaves so much more space for the good that awaits me. I pay bills promptly.

As I read this Hypnotic Narrative, I am aware that the words I see on this page are creating energy forms that are being created just for me. I feel my eyelids getting heavy as the power of these moments of creation becomes more real to me. I feel a warm, dreamy relaxation moving through my body as my eyes take in these words. I feel it now. And I know that this feeling brings with it the growing likelihood of my ideal outcome finding me. I repair broken things promptly.

As I continue to breathe deeply, I imagine myself moving or floating down a set of stairs. As I float down the stairs, I become more and more relaxed. I realize that I can reach an hypnotic state with my eyes open, even though it's becoming harder and harder to keep my eyes open as I become more and more relaxed. I get things done before they become worrisome.

As I continue to breathe deeply, I feel all cares and worries leave my body. I feel at peace and at ease, at one with the Universe and with my central goal. If I were to close my eyes for a moment, I could feel my energy coalescing with my ideal outcome. As my goal and I become one, the outer reality of that goal comes closer to fruition. I like knowing that things around the house work properly.

I can feel my body relaxing more and more. I service my car regularly. I realize that becoming or attracting whatever I want, is as easy as relaxing, opening myself to that possibility, and allowing that reality into my world. I have things that need attention as soon as I can. This new reality can feel a bit odd, new, and good all at the same time. I allow myself to sense the twinkle of happiness I feel about this ideal outcome. I allow myself to anticipate the pleasure that comes to myself and others as I reach my goal. I know that struggle is pointless and so unnecessary once I truly decide what I want, and simply invite the reality of taking immediate action into my life.

I truly look forward to improved health and improved relationships, now that I realize that struggle is needless and counter-productive to reaching my goal of getting free of procrastination. As I continue to allow myself to feel how good this new reality is for me, I commit to using my EOSH sessions daily to give this new reality even more life.

As I continue to breathe deeply, I feel myself expanding energetically, breathing freely, releasing any remaining old tensions, and moving closer and closer to achieving my ideal outcome. I repair broken things promptly.

As I continue to allow myself to become one with my goal, I have a sense of peace that seems to erase

any worries or fears I may have had awhile ago. I feel as if I've created a safe space in which to focus on achieving my goal without struggle or strife. I want this feeling of peace and inner quiet to stay with me throughout the day and decide to reinforce this wonderful feeling whenever you can today. I am looking forward to refocusing on my goals again and again throughout the day.

I am grateful to be able to enlist my inner genius to help me to achieve my goal. I like knowing that things around the house work properly. I am happy and confident that achieving my goal is right around the corner. I am certain that at my moment of perfect readiness, my goal will be achieved.

As I look around, I remember where I am. I smile to realize how deeply involved I've become in my EOSH Primary Hypnotic Narrative. My body feels relaxed; I have a sense of otherworldliness, sort of out of space and time. I feel good. I am happy to be alive and happy to be here and happy to be me. I am grateful for this experience and look forward to the next time.

211

I realize it's time to return to my outer reality. As I take a final deep and cleansing breath, I feel my attention and focus returning to the world around me. It's time to be back to reality and it's good to be back. I will keep watch today for all of the goodness that's headed my way.

CHAPTER 5

EYES OPEN HYPNOTIC DECLARATIONS

This chapter featured 88 Hypnotic Declaration Sessions which function as your EOSH Bonus Sessions. These quick sessions are used throughout the day as time allows, to reinforce the EOSH Primary Session you are working on. These declarative phrases are also an important part of the EOSH Primary session, in fact, these are the hypnotic suggestions that power your Primary session. Using these powerful phrases as your Bonus Sessions throughout the day deeply focuses your mind on your desired outcome.

When you review some of these declarations, your thought may be that the statements aren't currently true. You would be correct. The mental mechanism behind the use of these hypnotic declarations is to reinforce the changes you desire. They suggest and reinforce the changes that you want to transform your life. They are positive in nature and will replace any beliefs in lack or uncertainty about your ideal outcome that you may be temporarily holding in your mind. These are "manifesting" phrases, created to manifest your goal.

These phrases help to keep you focused on your ideal outcome. In this chapter, the specific session-topics that are starred have a corresponding EOSH Primary Session in the previous chapter, so if you see a starred session-topic that you want to use, go back to Chapter 4 to find it. The sessions in this chapter that are not starred can be added to the EOSH Primary Session Template included in Chapter 4 to create 58 additional EOSH Primary Bonus sessions.

For easy use away from your home, writing the appropriate series of EOSH Hypnotic affirmations in a notebook or inputting them into your smart phone, netbook, computer or tablet makes it as easy as possible to always have your EOSH Bonus session close to you. Next you will find your EOSH Bonus Session Hypnotic Affirmations grouped alphabetically under three separate categories: career, relationship, and general.

Remember, each starred session grouping has a corresponding Primary Bonus Session in the previous chapter.

CAREER SESSIONS

ACCOUNTING IS EASY

Math is easy for me.

I am becoming proficient at math.

I am grateful that accounting is so easy for me.

I enjoy improving my math skills.

I am comfortable with math.

I am a quick learner.

I love accounting.

BALANCING WORK & HOME*

I enjoy being at work and I enjoy being at home.

I balance my time and attention between home and work.

I am always mentally at home when I am home.

I look forward to going home at the end of the day.

I also look forward to returning to work.

I always balance both home and work.

The main reason I work is to support my family.

BEST FOOT FORWARD

First impressions count, so I make mine good.

I remember people's names easily.

I repeat a person's name several times after meeting.

I dress for success.

I take pride in my appearance.

216

I always look others in the eye.

I am always interested in what others are saying.

BEING APPRECIATED

I feel appreciated at work and at home.

I contribute fully at home and at my job.

I deserve appreciation and I enjoy it.

I enjoy being patted on the back.

I always do my best so I appreciate when others notice.

I enjoy being appreciated.

BECOMING A FREELANCER

Becoming a freelancer is coming closer every day.

I welcome opportunities and invite more into my life.

I am open to suggestions from others.

I am an independent thinker and love working on my own.

I am disciplined, so getting my work done is easy.

I enjoy a challenge and look forward to more challenges.

BRINGING YOUR "A" GAME CONSISTENTLY*

I love to work.

I love to do my best.

My self esteem is built in part on my doing a good job.

As I do my best, I profit myself and others.

Setting the bar high makes me a more valuable employee.

I respect those who perform their jobs professionally.

I enjoy being considered one of those people.

BUSINESS COMMUNICATION IS EASY

I enjoy keeping in contact with business associates.

Good business communication is essential to my success.

I strive to communicate as clearly as possible.

I pride myself on being a good communicator.

I stay up to date on the best ways to communicate in business.

I take business communication very seriously.

BUSINESS PROSPERITY*

My business is prosperous.

Money comes easily to me and to my company.

I love knowing that there is an infinite supply of money.

I attract money easily.

My business does better day by day.

I have complete faith in my business success.

I make sure that my customers are happy.

CAREER CHANGE IS EASY

I want a new career.

I invite all career opportunities.

I am open to opportunity.

I am excited by the thought of new responsibilities.

I expect a wonderful opportunity shortly.

I am the kind of person needed by many businesses.

I take my work seriously and give 100% to my job.

COMPUTER COMPETENCE

I am good with computers.

As I relax, computers are easier to deal with.

I enjoy learning more and more every day.

I am confident in my ability to use computers easily.

I appreciate how much time my computer saves me.

I am grateful to have a great computer.

CONFIDENCE AT WORK*

I am confident in my ability to do my job.

I know that I am a person who gives 100% to his job.

I am proud of the work that I do.

I enjoy contributing to my company and to society.

I know that I am highly regarded here at my
company.

I enjoy being praised for doing great work.

I feel that no one can do my job better than I can.

DEALING WITH CONFLICT*

I am a fair person.

I am fair to everyone I deal with.

I am easy to get along with and I avoid confrontation.

When confrontation is unavoidable, I deal with it calmly and fairly.

I never lose my temper because doing so is pointless.

In a conflict, the person who keeps his head and listens always wins.

DOING AN EMPLOYEE EVALUATION

When I evaluate an employee, I am fair and kind.

I choose to communicate honestly and kindly.

I tell the truth in a way that doesn't injure the employee.

I value the feelings of others.

I safeguard employees' feelings when possible.

I am patient, kind and honest with my employees.

DRESS FOR SUCCESS

I always dress for success.

I put my best foot forward in every situation.

I know that I only get to make one first impression.

I am fastidious about my personal grooming.

I respect others enough to strive to never offend.

My appearance helps me to move forward in the world.

I honor myself and who I am by dressing myself with care.

FIRING AN EMPLOYEE

I treat my employees with respect at all times.

When called upon to let an employee go, I am as kind as I can be.

I exude confidence in the employee's ability to find other work.

I share suggestions of where he might go for a new opportunity.

I thank him for his service to our company and wish him well.

I treat every employee as if he were a friend.

I fire others in the same way that I would choose to be fired.

GETTING A RAISE

I deserve a raise.

I am confident in approaching my boss.

I am prepared to explain why I deserve a raise.

I am equipped with statistics and proof.

I am courteous and never rude in my dealing with others.

I respect the person I am asking for a raise.

I am convinced that I deserve a raise.

GETTING FIRED & COPING

I chose to be courteous with the person who fired me.

I feel sorry for the person whose job it was to fire me.

I know I did my best, so I feel blameless in this process.

I look at this as an opportunity for bigger and better things.

Everything happens for a reason, even if the reason is yet unknown.

I look forward to exploring better opportunities.

READY FOR A PROMOTION

I want to be promoted to a better position.

I deserve a better position based on my work output.

I am certain my current skills will produce a new opportunity.

I know that I'm ready for bigger and better things.

I have enjoyed this job and look forward to new challenges.

I know that what is mine is moving toward me at this moment.

I trust that things are evolving perfectly.

GETTING RECOGNITION

I love being appreciated.

I work hard and love when others notice my efforts.

I am comfortable in the spotlight.

I enjoy compliments and praise.

Praise never embarrasses me.

I deserve the praise I receive.

GREAT SALESPERSON

I am a great salesperson.

I work hard to make sure that my customers are happy.

I pride myself on making good deals.

My company is happy with me.

My customers are happy with me.

I love it when the customer looks at me and says, YES!

I love being a salesperson.

JOB INTERVIEW CONFIDENCE

I love job interviews.

I see a job interview as a game that I want to win.

To win, I portray myself honestly and appealingly.

I love to win.

I am confident in my appeal and expect to be liked.

I have a work track record I am proud of.

I show up at a job interview well-prepared.

KNOWING YOUR WORTH

I am a valuable person.

I do good; I'm fair and honest.

I work hard and I treat others with respect.

I am courteous without fail.

I deserve respect and courtesy in return.

I require courtesy and respect.

I surround myself with other good people.

MAINTAINING BUSINESS INTEGRITY

I always do the right thing.

I treat customers and clients with respect.

I am honest to a fault.

I value what our company does and how we treat others.

I am proud to be someone who works ethically.

I only work with those who also have integrity.

MAINTAINING FOCUS

I am capable of easy focus.

I know the importance of focusing on the task at hand.

I am grateful to be blessed with a mind that can focus easily.

I am able to avoid distractions and accomplish the task at hand.

I am happy to focus while at work and to again focus at home.

Focus is a good thing.

MANAGING MULTIPLE PROJECTS AT ONCE

I am blessed with a mind that can handle many projects at one time.

I can be doing one thing and thinking about the next thing.

I multi-task easily and my work never suffers.

My mind is facile and capable.

Having a great mind is a major blessing.

I am grateful for the mind I have.

MANAGEMENT SKILLS

I am a natural manager.

People trust me and come to me to solve their issues.

I love that I am a person whom others trust.

I appreciate the respect I receive from others.

I am fair in my dealings with others.

I take my responsibilities very seriously.

I love what I do.

NEGOTIATING SUCCESSFULLY

I love to negotiate.

Many don't feel that way, but I am a natural.

Others trust me to work things out.

I save time and I save money for my company.

I am always fair and persuasive.

Fairness is the key to great negotiations, so I am unfailingly fair.

I enjoy a wonderful reputation as a great negotiator.

PUBLIC SPEAKING

I love public speaking!

I love to look at all the members of the audience one by one.

I always deliver a powerful, intelligent presentation.

I am never nervous or afraid.

Once I step up to the podium and begin speaking, I am ON!

I love to weave my words in ways that make total sense to the audience.

I love the applause I receive for a job well-done.

SHY NO MORE

I love meeting new people in new situations.

I have met so many fascinating people in so many places.

I love learning about others.

I love learning what their lives are like and where they live.

I have so much fun sharing information with new people.

I can tell they like me and that makes me happy.

Life is such an amazing adventure; I love it.

STARTING MY OWN BUSINESS

I am starting my own business.

I am excited to begin a new venture on my own.

I feel fully prepared to begin my business.

I have done my research and I've listened to my advisors.

I am looking forward to doing my own thing.

I am grateful for all I've learned in business and look forward to applying it.

I am happy to be starting my own business.

STAYING ORGANIZED IS EASY

I love to be organized.

I love knowing where the stapler is and the scissors.

I love knowing exactly where the files that I need are.

I realize the value of organization and embrace it.

I realize that I can be organized and still a free thinker.

Organization has become one of my major priorities.

STRESS FREE AT WORK

It's easy to stay relaxed at work.

The deadlines no longer stress me out.

I am always ahead of the game.

I am always prepared for whatever happens.

I pride myself on being prepared.

I love my work and I enjoy being here.

I get more done now than ever before.

WORK AT HOME NOW

I have always wanted to work at home.

My kids and family are there.

I know that the perfect opportunity is about to knock on my door.

I look forward to the freedom of working at home.

I anticipate the perfect opportunity to work at home.

I can imagine how good it feels to work at home.

WORK RELATIONSHIPS ARE EASY

I enjoy the people I work with.

I am pleasant and easy to get along with.

I am fond of most of my colleagues.

At work, I am relaxed and happy.

I am a team player and help out those who are buried in work.

I always greet everyone with a smile.

I am a cheerful person.

RELATIONSHIP SESSIONS

ATTRACTING THE PERFECT MATE*

My perfect mate is out there.

I am open to opportunities to connect with my mate.

I picture the perfect meeting with him/her.

I deserve the perfect mate.

I invite the Universe to send him/her to me.

There is room in my heart for my mate.

AVOIDING DIVORCE

I am willing to work on my marriage.

I forgive myself for inattention or unkindness.

I love my wife/husband.

I love my family and want us to stay together.

I forgive my wife/husband for real or imagined transgressions.

Our marriage matters.

I remember the person I married and want him/her back.

AVOID MARITAL TEMPTATION

I am an honorable person.

I am faithful to my spouse.

I sometimes find others attractive but I do not cheat.

Cheating on my partner cheapens me.

Cheating on my partner is dangerous.

I want our marriage to succeed.

I love my partner too much to hurt him/her this way.

DOORMAT NO MORE*

I am no longer willing to be treated disrespectfully.

I require others to treat me fairly.

I treat others fairly in return.

I am worthy of love and attention.

I am a person of value and appeal.

As long as I treat me kindly, so will others.

I am no longer a doormat.

FINDING YOUR SOULMATE

My soul-mate is out there.

I invite my soul-mate to find me.

I know that you're out there.

I want to share all my adventures with my soul-mate.

I am open and waiting for him/her.

Fill my heart with your loving attention.

Come to me now.

GREAT SEX*

I'm lucky to be an affectionate person.

I love to express my feelings with my body.

I love to touch the one I love.

Making love is natural and healing.

239

My body is very responsive to my lover.

Just the sight of my lover's body thrills me.

I love to touch and be touched.

HAPPY HOME*

I have a happy home filled with love.

I am lucky to be surrounded by love.

I put my family first.

I put my kid and husband/wife first.

They know that they matter to me.

I always look forward to coming home.

I take care of those I love and they take care of me.

HAPPY KIDS*

My kids are the best.

They are smart, funny, and beautiful.

Sometimes they try my patience but I love them anyway.

I am patient with my kids.

I always show my kids how much I love them.

I am proud of my children.

I respect my children's wishes whenever I can.

HAPPY MARRIAGE

My marriage comes first.

I love my job but when my wife/husband needs me, I'm there.

I put my partner first.

My husband/wife is my best friend.

I love to sleep next to my spouse.

I know what matters most in my life.

I honor my marriage vows every day.

I'M EASY TO GET ALONG WITH

I'm easy to get along with.

It matters to me that others like me.

Sometimes I put up with a lot to keep the peace.

I try to see the other person's point of view.

I am a very fair person.

I care genuinely for most people.

I consider myself a good person.

IN-LAW SUCCESS*

My in-laws are family.

My in-laws love my wife/husband and that's important.

My in-laws matter to my spouse so I get along with them.

My in-laws are generous with our kids.

Seeing them is always a pleasure.

I like my in-laws very much.

They are always kind to me.

MAKING FRIENDS EASILY*

I make new friends easily.

I love meeting new people and getting to know them.

I never hesitate to say hello to someone new.

I enjoy expanding my world to include new people.

People are fascinating and I love to hear their stories.

I really like people and people like me.

I take every opportunity to meet new people.

243

MAINTAINING YOUR INDIVIDUALITY IN MARRIAGE

I love my husband/wife and want him/her to be happy.

I am an individual as well as a partner.

My spouse understands my need to have my own interests/work.

My husband/wife is a very generous and secure person.

I take care of him/her and she/he takes care of me.

We can be united and still have separate interests.

Our separate interests make us each more interesting to each other.

MY KIDS GET ALONG WITH EACH OTHER

My kids are best friends.

They love to spend time together.

They share the same interests and entertain each other.

If one is in trouble, the other defends him/her.

My kids look out for each other.

They seldom disagree and never fight.

There is always peace in our house.

MY ADULT PARENTS

My parents and I are good friends.

I respect them and they respect me.

We have evolved into a strong and respectful relationship.

We each have our own space and respect that.

I am grateful to my parents for my upbringing.

I am grateful for their generosity.

I love my parents.

PERSONAL PAMPERING*

I love to be pampered.

I take every opportunity to be pampered.

I love to take care of my hair and my body.

I love to shop for beautiful clothes.

I take time for pampering.

I enjoy dressing up and going to a nice restaurant.

I always let my spouse pamper me.

PRIORITIES IN ORDER

I know what matters to me.

I am a good person and behave that way.

I take care of those I love.

I am respectful of those I love.

I am honest and honorable.

I am kind to strangers and always offer a helping hand.

I like who I am.

REMEMBERING WHO I MARRIED

I love the person I married.

I married a kind and loving person.

I married someone who pampers me.

I married someone who is interesting and fun.

I can still picture your face from all those years ago.

I remember why I married you.

I like you and I love you.

RESPECT & KINDNESS*

I deserve respect and kindness.

I offer respect and kindness to anyone I encounter.

I respect the rights of others.

I respect the rights of others to hold opinions that differ from mine.

I listen to the opinions of others courteously.

I am intentionally kind to everyone.

As I give respect and kindness, I receive it as well.

SEEING THE BEST IN OTHERS*

I choose to see the best in others.

I believe that most people are good.

I attract only good people into my life.

I am happy to see a silver lining in every cloud.

I believe that everything happens for a reason.

I believe that as I am kind, so is the world.

SINGLE & LOVING IT*

Being single is good.

Life is uncomplicated and simple.

There are no disagreements in a single household.

The best thing about being single is that everything is still possible.

A single person can meet the person of his/her dreams and act on it.

I love the freedom of being single.

I love not knowing what's around the next corner.

STANDING YOUR GROUND*

I can stand my ground peacefully.

It takes two to fight.

I am a strong, intelligent person capable of making decisions.

I have purview over my life.

I can assert myself pleasantly.

I can win when I want to.

I am a strong, competent person.

WORKING IT OUT- MARITAL NEGOTIATING

I always fight fair.

I am willing to give as well as take.

I am motivated by win-wins.

I always meet my partner half way.

I am easy to deal with.

I love figuring out how we can both win.

GENERAL

ACCESSING YOUR HIGHER POWER*

I am guided.

I am protected.

I have access to group consciousness.

I receive the information that I need.

I am connected to everyone and everything.

I am a light being.

I am blessed.

AGELESS*

I am not a number.

My chronological age is just a number.

I am who I choose to be.

I am the age I choose to be.

I am ageless.

251

I am eternally youthful.

CONFIDENCE BUILDER*

I am strong and brave.

I am competent.

I am capable of all tasks required of me.

I exude confidence.

I am confident in my abilities.

Everyone remarks how confident I am.

CONTROL ALCOHOL*

Alcohol has no hold on me.

I am free of any desire for alcohol.

Alcohol consumption is hard on my body.

I love the way my sober brain works.

I always do what's best for my body.

I love the way my sober body feels.

I love feeling strong and free.

CONTROL GAMBLING

I am free of the desire to gamble.

I am saving a lot of money.

I feel proud of myself.

My family is proud of me.

I can look myself in the mirror and feel good.

I can win only by no longer gambling.

EASY RELAXATION*

I am so lucky to be able to relax easily.

I can leave a hectic day behind easily.

My work day ends as soon as I get home.

I am patient with my children at all times.

253

My mind turns off when I tell it to.

I am able to play as hard as I work.

EXERCISE IS FUN*

Exercise is fun for me.

Exercise feels good.

I love the way my body feels when I exercise.

I know that exercise is good for my body.

I have fun no matter what kind of exercise I'm doing.

I look forward to exercising.

FEARLESS

I am fearless.

I am a strong, bold and confident person.

There is an inner ninja in me.

254

I know that I am always safe.

I keep my mind and body fit.

I value my physical strength and agility.

I see myself as a protector.

FITNESS MADE EASY

I love exercise equipment.

I love the way it looks and how it makes me feel.

My idea of fun is working out hard.

I love to feel my body react to a hard workout.

I love to build my body.

I love my body.

I AM ADVENTUROUS*

I am always up for a new adventure.

I am the first one to sign up for something new.

255

I feel safe in new situations.

I love new games, adventure vacations, and meeting new people.

There's nothing wrong with the norm, but the new is more interesting.

I like feeling a bit unsure in a new situation.

I like getting lost so I can get found.

I AM A RISK TAKER

Donald Trump and I are both risk takers.

If you have nothing to lose and something to gain, go for it.

The best fruit hangs from the highest branch on the tree.

Risk takers seldom have to settle for less than they want.

Being courageous and taking changes pays well.

Nothing ventured, nothing gained.

256

Go for it.

IMPROVED BALANCE

I move easily through the world.

I have perfect physical balance.

My inner ears function perfectly.

I feel as if I could safely perform a high wire act.

I move through life easily.

My body supports me perfectly.

IMPROVED DIGESTION*

My body digests food easily.

I eat, assimilate, and eliminate food optimally.

I choose to eat healthy food.

I have the digestive system of a young child.

I can eat like a horse and digest like one too.

My metabolism is excellent.

My entire digestive tract works perfectly.

IMPROVED EYESIGHT*

I have the eyesight of an eagle.

I am lucky to see so well.

I am careful with my eyes and try not to overtax them.

My eyes are my most valued possessions.

I love to see in the distance and up close.

Reading is a major pleasure for me.

I love my eyes.

IMPROVED HEARING

I can hear a pin drop in the next room.

I often hear conversations that don't involve me.

I am blessed with amazing hearing.

My ears work like they are brand new.

I value my ears and their excellent hearing.

I am grateful for fully functioning hearing.

IMMUNE SUPPORT

I have a healthy immune system.

I never get colds or flu.

I can't remember the last time I was ill.

My immune system supports my body perfectly.

I am grateful to have a strong immune system.

My immune system works perfectly.

LOSE WEIGHT NOW*

I enjoy foods that taste good and are good for me.

I enjoy salads, chicken and fish.

My digestive system works perfectly.

I digest, assimilate and eliminate like a healthy child.

My body releases excess weight and water easily.

My body is healthy and functions optimally.

I can eat what I want and still lose weight easily.

I release excess fat and excess fluid daily.

LIMITLESS

I choose to be limitless.

I embrace limitations that support a safe and healthy life.

I choose to use my mind and body to their fullest.

I appreciate my mind and my body.

I realize that my mind is infinitely powerful.

My life choices are many and I choose wisely.

MAKING FRIENDS EASILY*

Every person I meet is a potential new friend.

I really like people.

I enjoy meeting new people and learning about their lives.

People are fascinating.

I learn something new from everyone I meet.

I have time to share with many friends.

I love making new friends.

MEMORY BOOSTER*

I have an excellent memory.

I can remember phone numbers from my childhood.

I love trivia and jokes and remember tons of them.

I have the memory of an elephant.

I can place names to faces easily.

My mind is facile and remembers everything easily.

POSITIVITY BOOSTER

I am a happy, positive person.

I believe that everything happens for a reason.

I trust that everything is evolving perfectly.

I have a sunny disposition.

Others like to be around me because I am so positive.

I believe that a positive attitude contributes to good health.

PROCRASTINATION BE GONE*

I take care of things as soon as they show up.

I pay bills promptly.

I repair broken things promptly.

I get things done before they become worrisome.

I like knowing that things around the house work properly.

I service my car regularly.

I handle things as soon as I can.

PUBLIC SPEAKING IS FUN

I love to speak in front of a group.

I enjoy the excitement of sharing valuable information.

I enjoy feeling the audience respond to me.

I appreciate their smiles and nods.

I forget all about myself when I'm in front of a group.

I have total confidence in myself when I'm doing public speaking.

SEXUAL CONFIDENCE

I have total confidence in my ability to please my partner.

I pride myself on being a generous lover.

I delight in the sighs of pleasure my partner shares.

I attract others easily to me.

Others seem to feel my sexual confidence.

I am comfortable with new partners.

SLEEP EASILY

As soon as my head hits the pillow, I'm asleep.

I sleep easily and deeply.

I dream and I remember my dreams.

I enjoy going to bed because I love to go to sleep.

I leave any worries I have out of my bed.

When I go to sleep, I know that the next day will be wonderful.

I sleep like a baby.

SPEAK FOR YOURSELF

I speak up for myself.

I used to keep silent, but now I speak my piece.

I share my opinions kindly and firmly.

I know that I have the right to share my thoughts.

My thoughts and ideas are often valuable.

I feel comfortable sharing my thoughts with others.

I expect them to be received with interest and respect.

SPORTS SUCCESS

I am a natural athlete.

I can engage well in just about any sport.

I do well in competition with others.

I like to play hard and I love to win.

I know that with practice, I can do well with any sport.

I love to compete with others.

STOP SMOKING NOW

I am becoming smoke free now.

I am willingly and happily releasing that habit.

I look forward to smelling like a daisy.

I look forward to having a fresh tasting mouth.

I am willing and capable of living happily without smoking.

I am strong and once I make up my mind, that's it.

I love saving money and improving my health.

STRESS FREE NOW

I am relaxed and at ease.

I love the feeling of being relaxed.

I take the time to stretch whenever I feel tension arise.

I am strong and can handle anything.

My body relaxes naturally and easily.

I feel like I am a rubber band that can stretch and stretch.

STRONGER BONES

I am lucky to have such strong bones.

I have the bone density of a young woman.

My hair and nails are strong as well.

My body assimilates calcium properly and strengthens my bones.

My food nourishes my body and my bones.

Every step I take strengthens my bones.

STRONGER TEETH

My teeth are getting harder and stronger all the time.

The needed nutrients are available to my teeth.

I love my teeth and take care of them.

I realize the importance of my teeth.

My excellent digestion supports dental health.

I have beautiful teeth and I appreciate them.

THICKER HAIR

My hair is getting thicker all the time.

I have beautiful, healthy hair.

My hair is thick and full.

My hair is easy to manage and always looks good.

I am constantly growing new hair.

I love my hair

I hope you enjoyed this chapter and found a number of sessions you'd like to use as you begin your EOSH program. Remember that you have the choice of 88 session-topics by simply adding the EOSH Bonus hypnotic affirmations to the EOSH Primary Session template provided in Chapter 4.

And on to the final chapter with suggestions on how to maximize your success with the EOSH program.

CHAPTER 6

MAXIMIZE YOUR SUCCESS

Congratulations, you've reached the final chapter of *Eyes Open Self Hypnosis!* This last chapter is devoted to some final advice for the best ways for you to use the material you've discovered in *Eyes Open Self Hypnosis* plus my best wishes for your success!

SUGGESTIONS

First of all, being fully present as you use these sessions is important. Even if the laundry is waiting to be folded, focusing on these 2-10 minute EOSH sessions will make the difference between success and less than success. The laundry can wait a few moments. When you're using your primary EOSH session, please read it slowly, not necessarily in cadence but in a way that's similar to the cadence you will hear or have heard on your Free Audio EOSH General Narrative Session.

Speaking of the free session, consider playing that audio session once or twice daily for a few days. Listening to it several times will lock in a sense of relaxation that will transfer over to your own use of your primary session(s); it will also jumpstart the hypnotic process for you. Listening to it takes less than 8 minutes, and I think you'll find that time well-spent.

Get started now or as soon as possible. If you have 10 minutes right now and you're in a quiet place, use one of the EOSH Primary sessions now. You can finish reading this final chapter later. Feel how your body relaxes as you review your Primary Session Narrative. Enjoy the feeling because that feeling is moving you closer to your goal.

Even though I've offered some of these suggestions in an earlier chapter, here they are again.

EOSH PRIMARY SESSION NARRATIVES:

To begin your EOSH Primary Session Narrative, find a quiet spot where you can speak aloud or read quietly for 10 minutes or less. You don't need to be alone, but you do need to feel comfortable enough to allow yourself to enter a very relaxed state as you read your Hypnotic Narrative.

There's an advantage to using the EOSH primary session aloud for auditory learners. If you enjoy audio training programs and you use your Ipod daily, then hearing yourself speak the session out loud might heighten the experience for you. Whether speaking aloud or using it silently, you will accumulate added benefits every time you use your primary EOSH session, so whichever way you choose to experience it will be perfect. You might try speaking it aloud one day and the next time using your session silently. And using your Primary session one or more times daily whenever possible is really ideal!

If you have a lot of experience with meditation, guided imagery, and self hypnosis, you will feel increasing relaxation as you review your first EOSH primary session as early as that first session. If this is all new to you, be patient with yourself and the process, and expect very quickly to enjoy the benefits of increased relaxation and increased focus on your goal since your session will become more hypnotic every time you use it. Expect even quicker results as you become accustomed to the process.

Work on one Primary EOSH Narrative at a time, for at least 1 month. After a month, feel free to add an additional EOSH Primary Narrative to your existing program or to replace an existing program if you choose. Your subconscious mind is easily distracted, and since focusing on your ideal outcome is essential to achieving it, then focus on one goal. After a month of daily Primary EOSH sessions, your ideal outcome is firmly embedded into your inner reality, so adding a new Primary EOSH to the existing program is fine.

EOSH BONUS SESSIONS

Now let's look at your EOSH Bonus Sessions. As you know, the EOSH Bonus Sessions are just that; they are bonus opportunities to reinforce throughout the day, your primary EOSH ideal outcome. Your EOSH Bonus session is a short list of targeted, triggered hypnotic declarations that relate closely to your primary EOSH outcome. You can run through the selected group in 2-3 minutes, which allows you to review the Hypnotic declarations and also to picture yourself enjoying the results of your ideal outcome. The chapter on Hypnotic Declarations gives you some additional suggestions on the ideal use for these EOSH affirmations. You can add or change hypnotic declarations that you've included in your EOSH Bonus session at any time although I would recommend that you give the initial list at least a week of uninterrupted use to see the effect the initial group is having on your current reality.

A FANTASTIC EOSH DAY

A good *Eyes Open Self Hypnosis* day is one that has one primary EOSH session and an additional EOSH

Bonus session. A really good EOSH day has a primary EOSH session and 2 Bonus EOSH sessions. A great EOSH day has a primary EOSH session and 3 or more Bonus EOSH sessions. Remember the main point of the EOSH program is to keep your busy mind focused on your ideal outcome(s). EOSH Bonus sessions fit perfectly into a boring wait in line at the Post Office, the grocery store, or any time you have about 3 extra minutes to refocus on achieving your ideal outcome. Frankly, you can even fit several EOSH Bonus sessions into your workday without disrupting your work flow. And finally, a fantastic EOSH day is when you have listened to your EOSH Primary session played through headphones, and had 2 or more EOSH Bonus sessions or 2 traditional EOSH primary sessions and a bonus EOSH session. Whenever possible, aim for a Fantastic EOSH Day!

RECORDING YOUR EOSH PRIMARY SESSION

If you decide to record your EOSH session to maximize your results, that is really super! However, for those who don't want to record their sessions, be aware that recording a session is an upgraded use of the program and not essential to your success. Doing so may increase your enjoyment of the EOSH sessions and listening to the recorded session in a quiet place (definitely not driving the car) just once a week will speed the process of achieving your ideal outcome.

PROPS

I mentioned Props briefly in prior chapters. These are totally optional activities that you can use to further focus your mind on achieving your goals. Sometimes, doing something as simple as taping a picture that acts as a symbol of your goal can be really helpful. Every time you wash your face or brush your teeth, there it is for you to see. Taping your favorite EOSH Hypnotic Declaration in large print to the top of your mirror can also be effective.

If you want to own a particular car, for example, and that's what you're working on with your EOSH sessions, find a picture of that car in the color you want, cut it out and tape it somewhere in your house or at work, use it as a computer screensaver or place it wherever you look frequently. Visual aids are critical in educational programs, and EOSH is a re-educational program for your mind. Have fun with this program and wallpaper your Conscious Mind with images that represent your ideal outcome or goal!

If a slimmer body is your goal then posting in a prominent place, either a picture of a younger "you" with the body you want to recapture or the picture of a model with that body type will work great at helping your Subconscious Mind to remain focused on your ideal outcome.

Making a treasure map or a collage of images that represent the activities, objects or conditions that you want to manifest in your life can be a fun and powerful way to further reinforce your goal. Your collage can be made using a piece of copy paper and images that you find online that represent the changes you want to create in your life. It's a fun project to do with your kids if they are at an age where they will sit still long enough to work on their own

278

treasure maps. Any activity that provides more focus on the personal changes you want to make in your life can be valuable, and in this case, fun.

SUMMARY

Perhaps the most important first step is deciding what you want to work on first. The second step is getting started right now. The next step is making a commitment to your goal and to the use of your EOSH program as completely as your life allows, to maintain focus on that ideal outcome.

Thank you so much for reading this book. I really enjoyed writing it and I hope that you eek every ounce of goodness out of it that's possible. In this limitless world we all occupy, I will hold goodness and hope in my heart that each of you achieves all your hopes and dreams. Remember that you are limitless and as you choose to expand your possibilities energetically, so will your world expand.

If you have questions along the way, you can contact me through the NEIH website or through the website for this book, http://eyesopenselfhypnosis.com. This is also where you will find the link to your FREE

Bonus EOSH Primary General Session audio download.

If you enjoy this book and the process of EOSH, your feedback on the internet's largest retailer will be deeply appreciated. If you're still curious about traditional Self Hypnosis, please check out my other books, *Quantum Self Hypnosis* and *Quantum Hypnosis Scripts*. Please also check out my newest book, *Blueprint for Happiness*, written aboard the Royal Caribbean's Monarch of the Seas!

BIBLIOGRAPHY

Bartlett, Richard. *Matrix Energetics Reprint Edition.* Atria Books/Beyond Words, 2009

Chopra, Deepak. *Quantum Healing: Exploring the Frontiers of the Mind.* Bantam, 1990

Fezler, William D. *Creative Imagery-How to Visualize in all Five Senses.* Simon & Schuster, 1989

Fezler, William D. *Imagery for Healing, Knowledge & Power.* Fireside, 1990

Gawain, Shakti. *Creative Visualization.* New World Library, 2002

Lipton, Bruce. *The Biology of Belief.* Hay House, 2009

Robbins, Anthony. *Awaken the Giant Within.* Free Press, 1992

Ponder, Catherine. *Open Your Mind to Receive –New & Updated.* DeVorss & Co, 2007

Ponder, Catherine. *The Dynamic Laws of Prosperity.* Wilder Publications, 2009

Silva, Jose. *The Silva Mind Control Method* Pocket Books, 1991

Silva, Jose. *You the Healer: The World-Famous Silva Method on How to Heal Yourself and Others.* H.J.Kramer, 1992

Talbot, Michael. *The Holographic Universe*. Harper Perennial, 1999

Wolf, Fred Allen. *Taking the Quantum Leap*. Harper & Row, 1989

Made in the USA
Middletown, DE
06 September 2016